THE REFERENCE SHELF

Volume XII.

No.

1. **Anglo-American Agreement.** H. B. Summers. $1.25.

2. **Discussion Methods Explained and Illustrated.** J. V. Garland and C. F. Phillips. (rev. ed. 1940) $1.25.

3. **The State Sales Tax.** E. R. Nichols and others. $1.25.

4. **Dictatorships vs. Democracies.** 1938 (Supplement to Anglo-American Agreements) H. B. Summers and R. E. Summers. 75c.

No.

5. **Pump-priming Theory of Government Spending.** E. R. Nichols and William E. Roskam. $1.25.

6. **United States Foreign Policy: Isolation or Alliance.** J. E. Johnsen. $1.25.

7. **Chain Stores and Legislation.** Daniel Bloomfield. $1.25.

8. **The United States and War.** J. E. Johnsen.

9. **Debate Index.** E. M. Phelps. 75c.

10. **Radio Censorship.** H. B. Summers. $1.25.

Volume XI. $6

No.

1. **Unicameral Legislatures.** H. B. Summers.

2. **Consumers' Cooperatives.** J. E. Johnsen, J. V. Garland, C. F. Phillips.

3. **Industrial versus Craft Unionism.** J. E. Johnsen.

4. **Reorganization of the Supreme Court.** J. E. Johnsen.

5. **Unicameralism in Practice: The Nebraska Legislative System.** H. B. Summers.

No.

6. **Modern Group Discussion.** L. and E. Judson.

7. **Arbitration and the National Labor Relations Board.** E. R. Nichols and J. W. Logan.

8. **Peace and Rearmament.** J. E. Johnsen.

9. **Chinese-Japanese War, 1937-.** J. E. Johnsen.

10. **Representative American Speeches: 1937-1938.** A. C. Baird. $1.25.

Volume X. $4.20

No.

1. **Collective Bargaining.** J. E. Johnsen.

2. **Lotteries.** H. M. Muller.

3. **Old Age Pensions.** J. E. Johnsen.

5. **Socialization of Medicine.** J. E. Johnsen.

No.

6. **Limitation of Power of Supreme Court to Declare Acts of Congress Unconstitutional.** J. E. Johnsen.

9. **Government Ownership of Electric Utilities.** J. E. Johnsen.

10. **The Crisis in the Electric Utilities.** Garland and Phillips.

THE REFERENCE SHELF

Vol. 15   No. 5

THE "EIGHT POINTS"
OF POST-WAR WORLD
REORGANIZATION

COMPILED BY
JULIA E. JOHNSEN

NEW YORK
THE H. W. WILSON COMPANY
1942

PREFACE

The agreement, on August 1941, on an eight-point program —the so-called "Atlantic Charter"—by the British Prime Minister and the American President, has focused increasing attention on the fundamentals of a new world order which might reasonably be established at the end of the second World War. War and peace aims, the outlines of the international aspects of reconstruction, and more especially the foundations of a sound international order to supersede the disastrous nationalistic ideology of the past, have been discussed widely in recent years. With the promulgation of the eight proposed principles of a new order, enunciated by the two outstanding democratic statesmen of the world, a clear statement carrying official weight was for the first time presented as a proposed basis of civilization, designed to follow an Allied victory.

International federation and various other aspects of international organization were covered in an earlier number of the *Reference Shelf, International Federation of Democracies (Proposed)*, published in April, 1941. The present compilation is essentially a supplement to that number, and while it stresses the principles of international order as more recently expressed in the Atlantic Charter and materials on international federation appearing since the earlier publication, a somewhat broader survey has in it been attempted. For example, some mention is made of the proposed "new order" indicated by the Axis in the event of its ultimate success, and to some outstanding general programs and principles of post-war order and peace that have been enunciated, including America's relation to such a new international order.

Material on the Atlantic Charter, the eight points of which have been compared to the fourteen points of President Wilson in World War I, is as yet limited, although increasing. The broader international background and discussions will, therefore, afford additional helpful bases of measurement of the principles for a post-war world. For the convenience of debaters and others, bibliographical references have been classified (F) and (A) in various instances, indicating discussions for or against the aspects under which they are listed.

The compiler makes grateful ackowledgment for various courtesies in granting the use of copyright materials, which have made this compilation possible.

JULIA E. JOHNSEN

February 18, 1942

CONTENTS

DISCUSSION

THE ATLANTIC CHARTER [1]

It is becoming obvious to most of us that, whoever may be the victor in this war, the post-war world will be quite different economically, socially, and politically from that which our own and the few preceding generations have considered as normal.

The "shape of things to come," however, is beginning to form only vaguely for us. Nevertheless, if we cannot make definite prophecies, it is all the more important to follow such clues as we have. In this article we pick up the thread of only one, that leading from the meeting of the American President and the British Prime Minister in the Atlantic last August.

On their return, a statement signed by them jointly was given to the public, the wider implications of which are only gradually unfolding.

For example, when issued, it was called simply a statement of "Peace Aims," whereas now it is coming to be referred to as "the Atlantic Charter." One's mind runs back to Magna Carta, and the many charters in British and American history. The very word "charter" carries the connotation of something far more weighty and permanent than an "aim." Without ratification by the Senate or Congress as a whole, the full extent to which America may have been committed is open to question. But it may be noted that in foreign policy the President has enormous, if somewhat undefined, powers to lead the nation to a point from which it cannot turn back; and the course of events is often more influential than any of the three departments of government. That course is now flowing fast.

[1] By James Truslow Adams, Historian and Writer. *Barron's*. 21:3. October 13, 1941.

Another step was taken, with apparently friendly acquiescence from Washington, when representatives of nine nations, including Russia, met in London, and ratified the "Charter," making, according to the newspapers, eleven "Allies" adhering to the statement of aims which is on its way to becoming a "Pact." Without here discussing the wisdom for us of the proposed post-war role of the United States, we may consider briefly what may be some of the results if we do not retreat from the position assigned—a retreat becoming daily more difficult to make with honor.

In this connection there are several clauses especially to be considered. These provide, among other things, for the disarmament of any nations "which threaten, or may threaten, aggression outside of their frontiers"; for freedom of the seas; for "access, on equal terms, to the trade and to the raw materials of the world" by all nations, victors and vanquished; and for full collaboration among all in the economic field.

What do these clauses mean? For one thing, from the text itself and later comments by Churchill, Secretary Knox and others, they must mean that "pending the establishment of a wider and permanent system of general security," America and the Empire make themselves primarily responsible for keeping potential aggressors disarmed and for policing the world by sea and land.

What does this mean economically? In the first place it means that for an indefinite period we must remain, even after peace, on a war or semi-war footing. It means a new set-up of industry; plants built or altered for "the emergency" would, to an unexpectedly large extent, remain in production for an arms industry which would normally shrink to nominal proportions when war was over. This would have a tremendous effect on wages, employment, production, and prices.

There would be another important effect. After the Civil War we had the riches from the development of the West to draw on. After the first World War we had the enormous profits we had made from it, so that we reduced the government debt by $9 billion, far more than a third, in 11 years. The new arms industry here envisaged would differ from other industries in that it would be government paid-for. It would hinder reduction of either debt or taxes, and so have its effects on earnings of other industries and on government finance. If the government debt, starting at, say, $75 billion to $100 billion at the end of the war, is not reduced but tends to increase, we must consider the effects on insurance companies, savings and other banks, and private funds. Also it means heavy inflation.

There are other points. If all nations "great or small," as the Charter states, are to have "access on equal terms" to the trade and materials of the world, it could seem to mean only that the whole present and complicated system of tariffs and other nationalistic hindrances to trade would have to be scrapped. This has not yet proved feasible even within the Empire itself as between England and the Dominions. Furthermore, such wholesale readjustment all at once of present world trade could not be made without such shifts in prices, wages, production, trade routes, and all the rest, as to make the future of any particular industry, group, class, even nation, almost unpredictable, even provided that all would be willing to be self-sacrificing enough to make the attempt.

The Charter says that the purpose would be that of "securing, for all, improved labor standards, economic adjustment and social security," but although I, for one, have believed our tariffs much too high and one of the causes of the depression of the 'thirties, I doubt whether America could be induced suddenly to give all nations "access, on equal terms," to our trade, and whether our labor standards or security would be improved if we did so. It may be that I misunderstand the words of the Charter, though they seem clear enough. To bring world prices —for goods and labor both—all to one level would cause intense maladjustment, would bring suffering in the present high-priced countries, and virtually give the fruits of the war to the totalitarian instead of to the democratic nations.

But there are also other tasks outlined for us. The belief is growing that the Charter involves stabilization of the world's currencies, "a consummation," in Hamlet's phrase, "devoutly to be wished," but one which I see no hope for except in the re-establishment of the gold standard. Trade on equal terms for all nations cannot be had with each nation edging in for an advantage by depreciating its paper money. Perhaps the answer may be the plan advocated by our Assistant Secretary of State, Berle, last year when he suggested that we might be called on to give a part of our huge and unwanted gold hoard as a free gift to other nations for the purpose of putting them again "on gold." But if so, there is another unpredictable economic effect of the Charter which it will behoove all to consider.

An additional problem was raised when, at the London Conference mentioned above it was resolved that all the nations which had assented to the Charter would join in feeding Europe after the war. This will probably have to be done, not merely for humanitarian reasons but to achieve any sort of settled world. Nevertheless, the economic consequences on our crop surpluses, farm policies and government finance may well be considered. It is true that this promise is not one of the eight "aims," but as we have said, the Charter is already being altered and expanded. As one observer said at the September meeting in London, "the fact that all these nations with so many different aims could afford to pledge themselves so unreservedly was an indication of how vague and general the Atlantic Charter had been made."

The Charter *is* vague, but, on the other hand, unless one is to ignore the plain implication of its words there is enough in it if the words are honest and mean anything, to cause us all to ponder the consequences somewhat along the lines suggested above or others.

For instance, Secretary Knox in his address of October 1, said: "To put it bluntly, we must join our force, our power to that of Great Britain, another great peace-loving nation, to stop aggression which might lead to a world disturbance, at its beginnings." We must, he continued, not only defeat Hitler (and Italy and Japan) but prevent the rise of new Hitlers or other dictators. We must, for an interregnum of "a hundred years," he suggests, instruct the world in the fundamentals of international law.

Certain things occur to one. Germany was supposed to be disarmed after the Treaty of Versailles, yet secretly she rearmed with the result from which we are suffering today and which threatens the end of civilization. Obviously, it would seem that more than navies, with their air forces, must be maintained by us and the Empire for the next century if we are to police the world for that period, and to prevent (which means to "come before"), another sabotage of international law or an attempt by some nations against the safety of others. Such an undertaking would seem to mean not only patrolling the seas but internally policing Germany, Italy, Japan, and perhaps other nations now unrecognized, numbering several hundred millions of people.

We might also ask, What about Vichy or some new France? And what about those nations which, although now opposed to Nazi domination, might also object to a world controlled by an Anglo-American alliance? It may be true, as Secretary Knox says, that "the only kind of peace which is available . . . is the kind of peace that can and will be enforced through the superior power of those nations that love justice and seek after peace." Suppose Russia and other countries should say "we have our own ideas of justice and they do not agree with what the Americans and British decide must be enforced against us." To keep the seas "clear of pirates in the future" is, as Knox also says, a very great responsibility, but to enforce our ideas of peace and justice over all the two billions of the earth's inhabitants outside the

States and the Empire would make our responsibility "very great" indeed!

How would this be done? And could America, with its isolationist and pacifist traditions, be induced to follow this road to an unknown destiny? The peace-loving, freedom-loving peoples are evidently groping toward some means which will prevent a return to barbarism, a reign of brute force, and the loss of that freedom of mind and spirit which now threaten us. There is the problem, however, of how far in a rapidly filling and restive world peace can be combined with a more or less rigid *status quo,* and there is also unhappily a wide gulf between the essential or desirable and the possible in human affairs. From the standpoint of the democracies and of civilization, as we envisage it, the defeat of Germany, Italy and Japan is essential. But then what? That interrogation is perhaps to be followed by the biggest question mark in all human history. If the second World War, like the first, results in no established order, even for a while, then, as the Doughboys used to say in France in 1918, "where do we go from here?"

To come back to the Atlantic Charter. However vague it may be, a careful consideration of it may have one important result. I was at the last Peace Conference in Paris for months, after having spent five earlier months in a modest capacity helping to prepare the data for it. I know something of the difficulty of making a peace—the infinite intricacy of the multitudinous and widely ramifying problems involved, the passions of the peoples at home, the need for haste lest revolutions flood the world again with blood, the personalities of the negotiators. The settlement of the present war, even if the Allies win definitely, will be the most complicated problem the human mind has ever had to solve.

One thing is certain, whatever the Atlantic Charter may mean, and however its eight clauses may or may not be invoked specifically, the old world we knew is dead and what the new one may be we do not know. If it is to be one in which free men will care to live, they will have to make sacrifices and put away prejudices. Events will do it for us if we do not do it willingly and intelligently ourselves. It may be a world in which both martial law and the spirit of charity will have to be exercised for years.

In my opinion the only two nations which are capable of doing the job are the United States and the British Empire. I want no union of them other than of hearts and aims and collaboration in the work of rebuilding a world in which the liberty they have both clung to throughout their histories may be restored. If we cannot do it—and we can do it only in working together—then no one can do it, and darkness will again be on the face of the deep.

There are more than economic implications to the Charter. We may not agree with the answers it gives, but we cannot, except at our peril, ignore the questions it propounds.

DILEMMAS FOR A POST-WAR WORLD [2]

If economics means utilization of resources for human welfare, war can hardly have economic causes. Certainly the utilization of resources for war is not the utilization of resources for human welfare. If, however, economics means utilization of resources for any purpose whatever, including utilization for the purpose of building up political power, then obviously there may be economic causes of war. The prime cause, however, would lie in the realm of politics. One would have to ask why a government or a people wants to build up political power. One reason is that centralization of political power appears superficially to be the best way to maintain order. This, however, overlooks the fact that permanent order cannot neglect justice and that too great a centralization of power would inevitably do

[2] By Quincy Wright, Professor of International Law, University of Chicago. *Free World*. 1:14-16. October, 1941.

so. Effective organization is not achieved by centralized power, but rather by the maintenance of equilibrium. Fundamentally, politics is the process of adjusting divergent opinions concerning government. The process is one of adjustment and compromise, rather than of command. In this sense the process of politics consists of continually resolving dilemmas neither horn of which can ever be entirely rejected.

One of these is the dilemma between peace and justice. Lord Halifax, as British representative on the League of Nations Council, suggested that recognition of Mussolini's conquest of Ethiopia, although contrary to abstract ideas of justice, should be accepted as an immediate victory for peace. The Emperor Haile Selassie, on the other hand, said that the League of Nations was not free to subordinate justice to peace and that he feared a policy with this objective would achieve neither justice nor peace. Subsequent efforts of statesmen to preserve peace by repeatedly sacrificing justice to appeasement give a good deal of support to the Emperor's contention. Justice and peace are both worthy ideals and the world should be so organized that statesmen are not often presented with the dilemma of choosing between them. This can be done only by organizing a genuine community of nations with such solidarity that adequate force can be relied upon to support justice. A successful international organization must always have in mind Pascal's thought, "Justice without force is powerless, force without justice is tyrannic."

Another frequently presented dilemma is that between political power and efficient administration. Psychological studies have indicated that the human characteristics that make it possible for an individual to achieve leadership and political power in a community are not necessarily accompanied by the capacities that make for efficient administration. Effective political organization requires a government with enough power to administer and enough intelligence to administer well. It is hard to set up a system that will assure a government personnel with both these qualifications. Democracy, in which power rests upon the support of public opinion, cannot be successful unless it recognizes the need for administrators selected because of their skill, and the need, especially in times of emergency, of leaving them a considerable sphere of free activity.

Then there is the dilemma that exists between the demands of timing and those of progress. There are occasions when delay and opportunity to think things over will in themselves solve dangerous controversies. On the other hand, there are times when delay will make controversies worse. Delay may, in fact, destroy stability altogether. Revolution and war, from one point of view, may be considered an effort to make progress too rapidly. On the other hand, failure to act may on occasion be the very cause of violence. There is no art of statesmanship more important than that of properly estimating the time element and relating it to the means of change in a given situation. Successful political organization involves institutions which make for delay in situations where too rapid action is dangerous and which facilitate action in situations where delay is dangerous.

Still another dilemma is to be found between area and function. In the situation that will confront the world after the war a sound solution of this dilemma will be most necessary. On the one hand, a sound political organization should control a geographical area wide enough to make feasible the full and effective exercise of its administrative functions; on the other hand a political organization should be confined to a geographical area within which there is a certain homogeneity of opinion. In our era of world-wide communications a political organization as wide as the world would seem to be called for; but the intensity of national sentiment suggests that political organizations still can be no larger than the nation. Between the movement for international organization and the movement for national self-determination, the first concerned primarily with the problems of government and the second emphasizing the homogeneity of public opinion, there is obviously a serious dilemma. Certainly under present conditions a world attributing absolute sovereignty to the nation-state cannot be a world at peace. Such a world prevents the efficient use of resources for human welfare. It continually stimulates the nation-states to expand into empires which they hope will give them the resources they need. But since there are not empires enough to satisfy all, war is bound to result. The solution can only be found in a complicated federalized system in which at least five areas of political jurisdiction are recognized and the functions of government properly distributed among them.

The smallest of these areas is the individual, who should have certain fundamental rights guaranteed by the world order. A nation that so controls the opinion of its members that they are cut off from communication with their fellow human beings in other sections of the world is dangerous. Freedom of speech, of the press, and of religion are safeguards against the building of dangerous totalitarian states. Some freedoms in the economic sphere are also necessary. It is worth remembering that the nineteenth century, in which the system of economic liberalism flourished as never before, was the most peaceful century Western civilization has known, at least since the Pax Romana. Economic planning by a political group that is less than universal makes political boundaries into economic boundaries and increases the strain upon them. On the other hand, it is difficult to build a universal planning agency with sufficient power to control the economic activity of individuals without at the same time controlling public opinion. And this is only possible when individuals are willing to subordinate themselves because of the fear of external invasion or some other profound form of pressure. Historically there is much to support Walter Lippmann's assertion that the socialistic state is necessarily poor and bellicose. The solution of the economic problem would seem to lie not in the governmentalization of economy but in improvement of the automatic system by which production is controlled by the choice of the individual consumer through a market mechanism.

While protecting basic rights of the individual, however, rights of local communities, of nations, of continental regions, and of the world as a whole must not be neglected. It is impossible here to set forth the functions which should be attributed to each of these areas. Local communities should be free to develop local services for their citizens. The nations should have sufficient autonomy to develop their cultural peculiarities, arts, and customs. It appears that the functions of police and defense should pass from the nation-state to the region. Invention of the airplane has made it impossible for a small nation-state to enjoy any security under a balance of power system. Before this invention, such a state, with moderate military equipment and the expectation of assistance from great neighbors operating under the balance of power concept, could defend itself against the aggressions of even a powerful neighbor. With the airplane, however, the powerful aggressor can overcome its weak neighbors in days or even hours.

Europe might organize as a confederation with a military and air police more powerful than the force of any of the member states. Such a confederation should recognize the full cultural autonomy of the nations and should rest upon an equilibrium of the Slavic, Latin, and Germanic peoples, so that no one could dominate the rest. Other great regions of the world should also be organized for security on a basis adapted to the particular conditions of the region. Oceanic areas might be similarly organized for certain purposes, and a state might even find it advantageous to participate in more than one of these regional groupings.

Continental areas, if organized independently, would probably seek to become self-sufficient and to acquire external areas producing essential foodstuffs or raw materials. Imperialism and war would then flourish on an even grander scale. Regional federations and their member states should therefore be organized within a looser world federation that would control and insure moderate freedom of trade, protect basic individual and

national rights, and, through control of sea power and naval
aviation, insure pacific settlement of inter-regional controversies
and support the regional organizations in dealing with intra-
regional controversies. The Pact of Paris, the League of Nations,
and the Permanent Court of International Justice may provide
the basis for such an organization.

The experience of the British Empire during the past century
indicates the naturalness and wisdom of a close federation of
contiguous political areas coupled with a looser organization of
the federations separated by oceans. The architects of a new
world organization should bear this historic precedent in mind.
A world organization would be primarily concerned with juristic,
economic, financial, and maritime affairs. It might assume responsibility for the development and eventual self-determination
of colonial areas, assuring in the meantime equal access to their
resources by all nations.

To achieve equilibrium among these five political groupings
will not be easy. The breakdown of the political structures of
the past as a result of the agressions of the totalitarian powers,
may, however, facilitate such a reorganization. The central problem will be Europe and the central thought must be a European
union with sufficient power to preserve peace and to support
justice with sanctions. That power must, however, be limited
from below by guarantees of the rights of nations and of individuals, and it must be limited from above by the demands
of a world organization. The powers and functions which in the
past have belonged to the governments of sovereign nation-states
must be distributed among these various orders in the political
structure of the new Europe.

The situation is not unlike that of the fifteenth century, when
the medieval system was coming to an end. The invention of
the gun at that time made the previously invulnerable feudal
castles no longer defensible. A new order was created by the
unification of thousands of feudal principalities into nation-states.
These units facilitated not only political but also economic de-

velopment. Inventions of our day have in turn made these national units too small. Two world wars have demonstrated the failure of this system of sovereign states controlled only by a balance of power. In 1920 we witnessed progress in the formation of the League of Nations, but we witnessed also the incapacity of statesmen, especially on this side of the water, to realize the necessity of making the League work. If the opportunity is presented again, democratic statesmanship must not only perceive the problem but must also act to solve it. It cannot do this unless democratic public opinion itself realizes the problem and envisions the broad direction of the solution. Such an enlightenment of public opinion should be the function of organizations devoting themselves to the cause of a free world. Peace and freedom in our present world are simply different words for the adequate political organization of the world as a whole and of its various regions, nationalities, and localities. To assure the maximum welfare for human individuals, democracy must not forget its basic tenet: that government exists for the individual, whether viewed as a distinctive personality or as a morally responsible member of society.

THE POLITICAL BASIS OF FEDERATION [3]

A predominant note in the speculations of liberal-democratic thinkers on the subject of post-war reconstruction has been an insistence on the need for "some kind of a federation." As a popular catch-word, "federation" has undoubted propagandist value. It has come to acquire some of the magic properties once associated with phrases like "a parliament of man," "league of nations," and "outlawry of war." For the pamphleteer and orator, therefore, it is a ready-made formula which should be fully exploited for the purpose of engendering a readiness for international collaboration.   •

[3] By William P. Maddox, Associate Professor of Political Science, University of Pennsylvania. *American Political Science Review*. 35:1120-7. December, 1941.

In a general sort of way, we can grasp the federal idea as a response of the mind to the political problem of the one and the many—of the need for achieving both unity and diversity, order and liberty, centralization and autonomy—in the composing of human affairs. Nevertheless, there is need for a critical examination of "federation" as a political principle or system, of the circumstances out of which federations have arisen and can arise and of the conditions of their successful operation. In these few pages, an attempt will be made to indicate a few types of theoretical and historical investigation which may, it is hoped, prove stimulating in the quest for understanding.

Analysis of the basis of federation is impeded, at the outset, by the apparent ambiguity of the concept. The common elements in the political structures of the United States, Canada, Australia, Switzerland, South Africa, the Germany of Bismarck and of the Weimar Republic, are extremely elusive. General usage sanctions application of the term "federal" to their governmental forms, but some opposition is raised to the inclusion of some of the inter-city associations of the Hellenic world, or the present U.S.S.R., or the Argentine, Venezuela, and several other Latin-American republics. Etymology is even more confusing, since the Latin *foedus* conveys a sense much less extensive than normally covered today by "federation." An examination of authorities shows a studied evasion of sharp definition, and much elaboration of qualifications, exceptions, and variations.

But political scientists are never unduly dismayed at having to talk about something the meaning of which no two can agree on. Most of the general concepts with which they have to deal are no less fluid in their textual composition. Here, however, one may resort to the logical device of conceptual extremities linked by continuous gradations. At one end of an imaginary line may be posited the idea of an absolute, unitary world-state, and at the other the conception of complete anarchy—a number of disconnected units in a condition akin to Hobbes' fictional state of nature. The extremities are always conceptual, never actual, and any given period of international relations may be charted some-where between, along a sliding scale. Starting from the state of anarchy, one imagines, in succession along the line, a nebulous international law, the development of voluntary institutions and procedures, then a confederation, next a federation, and on and on, and finally, the emerging condition of a world-state. No sharp line separates one from the other—for instance, a confed-eration from a federation—but rather twilight shadings to con-found the pedant. (Indeed, one may expand the conceptual structure into a two-dimensional form to introduce other notions varying from an absolute master-slave relationship to absolute equality, but, for the moment, there is need for simplicity rather than complexity.)

At the exact center of this conceptual series may be placed the pure idea of federation—a perfect balance or compromise between the extremes: a form of political organization which represents a compounding of separate units in such a manner that a central authority prevails in the sphere of common concern, and the several autonomous authorities in the sphere of partial concern. At some indefinite point moving off to the one side of this conceptual pivot, the central authority would become so powerful and extensive that the individual parts would become subordinate, and a unitary form of government would develop; equally, in the other direction, the point would be reached where the central power would cease to exercise an independent will and become a mere servant of the local governments, and thereupon federation would fade into a confederation or a league. Without laboring verbal distinctions, it must be repeated that the essential feature of federation is the existence of two focal areas of politi-cal will—the central which controls the aggregate of individuals in their entirety, and the several local ones which govern au-tonomously in their respective territorial sub-divisions. Behind both must exist a constitutional understanding defining the spheres of authority.

But, it may be asked, is not all this mere pedantry? Of what avail is such an exercise in political logic for the liberal-democratic planners of a new world order? Do we not, in the practical world of political action, tend to create first, and let the academicians legitimatize the offspring with an appropriate name afterwards? Without denying the practice, one may still question its social desirability. Much would be gained even if a clear comprehension of the essential nature of federation should lead to a total rejection of the idea in thinking about international reconstruction. We should then be better equipped for planning a more realistic alternative.

So much for definition. Now, federation may develop as a result either from a centrifugal political force—the breaking down of a unitary form of government; or from centripetal action—the building up of parts into a new entity. The former is obviously of no value in the quest for light on international relations, and it is to the latter that we turn. Here arise two fundamental questions: (1) What are the propulsions making for centripetal action leading to federation? and (2) What are the conditions upon which an effective federation can be maintained?

The most important forces of a political, or psychological, order which serve as efficient agents in the creation of federation are fear, a calculated expectation of advantage, and a response to some unifying ideal or myth. Of these three, the most important motivation is probably fear. Fear may develop from direct attempts at intimidation, or from a sustained and profound feeling of insecurity. Intimidation, shading into actual coercion, may be undertaken by a strong political unit seeking to obtain the adherence of weaker units under a nominal federal form. The term is too strong to apply to the methods by which overwhelmingly predominant Prussia initiated, first, the North German Confederation of 1867, and second, the Empire of 1871; but the smaller states of Germany were thoroughly aware of Bismarck's indomitable purpose to achieve union no matter what

the cost. "A more extensive union of the majority of Germans,"
said he in 1868, "could be obtained only by force—or else if
common danger should arouse them to fury." The former alternative did not become necessary, since the latter intervened.
The method of intimidation of the weak by the strong is not
recommended to the architects of international federation, but in
extreme cases it may present the only feasible alternative if
union be deemed a supreme necessity.

A sustained and profound sense of insecurity has proved a
most efficient agent for social and political integration, and advocates of international federation do well to recognize that fact.
The insecurity may be political—the fear of invasion, war, or
rebellion; or economic and financial—the fear of panic and
starvation. Financial fears contributed to the successful efforts of
the Philadelphia Convention of 1787; and political danger (encountered in the Franco-Prussian War) to the Empire of 1871.
Where the danger is visualized as concrete and external to the
federating groups, its integrating power is far greater than if the
menace is conceived abstractly as some indeterminate aggression
within the projected association. Unity, in other words, is
cemented by specific, external opposition. Thereby is indicated
an inherent weakness in any plan to establish universal federation
all at one stroke. All that it can promise is the curbing of some
unnamed political enemy within. If that enemy be clearly indicated, why should he unite with the others? If no enemy be
clearly indicated, the danger is too remote, contingent, and
unpredictable for any to find need to unite.

A possibility remains that the imminent prospect of world-
wide economic collapse may prove an effective incentive to union.
In facing such disaster, however, the position of some would
undoubtedly be stronger than that of others; the fear and hope
would be of uneven intensity. The strong are than disinclined to
encumber themselves with the problems of the weak; a partial
federation may be facilitated, but a universal union may be far
off in realization.

Again, where insecurity is not felt strongly, there is little incentive to undertake more extensive obligations. A firm belief in its ability to take care of its own defense and economic problems has for decades kept the United States in its policy of isolation. In the years already upon us, that confidence has been rudely shaken, and Federal Union advocates have correctly gauged the importance of that fact. Only when isolation comes to be regarded as a greater danger than union, only when it becomes unmistakably evident that comfortable existence cannot be maintained through independence, will the impulse to federation become strong enough to be translated into action.

Having said that, only a word is needed with regard to the other possible motivations for the act of federating. A rational calculation of advantage is important and certainly must play a part in the appeal to the practical, hard-headed class of voters. In the United States, the *Federalist* papers stand as eloquent testimony to the utility of this type of approach. Likewise, the desirability of evoking some unifying ideal, symbol, or myth cannot be overlooked. Here the word "federation" itself supplies the need for those long accustomed to its meaning and practice. The idea of an English-speaking unity, or that of a Union of Democracies, might have even greater force. Unfortunately for the leaders of the Pan-European movement, the geographical contiguity has had no electrifying appeal—certainly not as against the deep-rooted divisions on that continent. Since the disappearance of the unity of Christendom, no universal myth has appeared sufficient in power to unite all classes and races of humanity, although some have urged that "peace" or "social justice" might at some distant day supply that force.

It may be said, in summary, that in founding an international federation, the propulsions of political and/or economic insecurity are believed to be absolutely indispensable, and a rational expectation of gain, along with a unifying ideal, of secondary (but nevertheless great) importance.

Even if some overwhelming fear psychosis should provide a propulsion sufficient for the creation of a federal structure, it does not provide a sustaining power over the long haul. For effective operation, the federal union must discover an enduring as well as a generating basis. Some of the problems may be indicated. *16512*

First, the parts of the federation must not represent too great a diversity in size, culture, and the level of their political and economic development. Contrast in size is probably of least importance, although one may well argue that the unusual predominance of Prussia undermined the federal structure of Germany. Even in a league, there are disadvantages, as the example of Athens in the first Athenian League testifies. Internationally, however, the ratio which the population of the United States bears (for instance) to New Zealand is not as great as that of the state of New York to that of Nevada. Sharp differences in the levels of culture and of economic and political development are another matter. The project for European union has to contend with the difficult problem of linking together in common life on a basis of equality the undeveloped peoples of southeastern Europe with the advanced communities of the northwestern part of the continent. And international federation (whatever its constituency) would certainly have to maintain a superordinate trusteeship over most of Africa and part of Asia, at the least—all sentimentalism to the contrary. So far as this factor is concerned, the proposal for the Federal Union of the Democracies has an undisputed advantage over other projects.

Second, geographical contiguity is unquestionably desirable. All existing national federations possess such contiguity, and it is a most compelling argument for European and other continental unions. Part of its advantage has to do with compactness for defense purposes, part for the similarity of internal problems, and part for the practicability of legislative assemblage and administrative controls. The plan for the union of America and the British Commonwealth raises defense problems of sea power, which are not insoluble. Such a union could not possess an effective land force on the continents of Europe and Asia, and should only be extended to include countries in those regions which can find a means of continental defense. Common assemblage in a union parliament and the establishment of some central administrative control present problems far more difficult for the British-American plan than for a continental federation. It is too much to say that geographical obstacles render such a plan unworkable, but they suggest that the degree of federal unification and power cannot be too extensive.

Third, unifying forces of a spiritual, emotional, or ideological character not only contribute to the formation of union but give it sustenance and vigor in its struggle for survival. While useful at the time of emergence of union, their strength may be increased through the slow crucible of common experience—governmental, administrative, social, economic, and intellectual. Thus the myths of the American Union have grown slowly over a century and a half, and the fusion of the parts of the Union has been a correspondingly gradual process.

Finally, we must consider the problem of the sources from which the central government of a federation may derive its power. There is no true federation, it will be remembered, unless the central authority possesses a power of decision and action independent of the wills of the separate governments. Briand's plan for European Union, involving a sort of council of governmental delegates acting under instructions from home, was certainly not a federal conception. One of the most widespread misconceptions about international federation is that it may result from, or be sustained by, a simple abdication of sovereignty on the part of independent governments. In the first place, national governments cannot, and will not, transfer their sovereignty to an agency which is only defined on paper. In the second place, if the power of the central organs emanates solely from such authority as each governmental subdivision grants, then that central will is subordinate to the separate wills—at least in their aggregate. Even though majority procedures be substituted for those of unanimity, a dissentient minority could withdraw or terminate its contribution of men, money, materials, and other instruments of power at any time. The inherent weakness of a league or confederation would not have been overcome.

The government of a federation must, therefore, develop its power from sources (at least in part) independent of the national governments. The bases of power in this connection are threefold: political (or representative), financial, and military. Policymaking officials of the central government must (at least in part) be chosen by direct or indirect election. There can be no such thing as a federation which includes totalitarian régimes denying free political action. The American Constitution recognized the necessity for instituting direct and indirect elections instead of appointments by the executive power of the several state governments. Bismarck's decision to advocate a national German parliament elected by universal franchise resulted from his clear recognition of the need for generating a political force strong enough to override state particularism. The development of political parties across state frontier lines is thus facilitated, and this development in turn provides a new unifying basis for the federation. Again, the proposal for a Federal Union of the Democracies has seized hold of an essential attribute of federation. There can be a real federation only where domestic conditions permit the organization of people in their private capacities, the holding of free elections, and the maintenance of representative institutions. Only thus could an independent basis for the power of the federation's central government be obtained.

The second basis of power is financial, and that also must come from the people through the power of direct taxation, rather than through the device of levies upon state governments.

Given financial independence, the third basis—military power —can also be found in the people through direct recruitment and organization of personnel. Moreover, the central government must, through this independent force, maintain a military monopoly. It should be noted again at this point that the implications of the "Streit plan" differ sharply from those of continental or world federation. Democratic Union advocates do not conceive the military function as that primarily of preventing civil war, but of consolidating forces for defense against some enemy without. European, or world, federation, on the other hand, is generally thought of as a device for curbing some aggressor within the association. It should be unmistakably clear that the union of democracies on this score faces an easier task because of its greater cohesion.

The foregoing observations were not prepared as a brief for or against any particular project for international organization. Their purpose is simply to suggest the need for a more thorough-going analysis of a concept which has been so frequently and loosely employed in the literature of liberal-democratic world planning. All of this speculation will, of course, have been utterly futile if the Axis triumphs, since no opportunity will be provided for the free association of peoples. In the event of British (or, it may be, an Anglo-American) victory, at least a strong probability exists that the federal idea, or some diluted form thereof, will receive favorable attention in the task of political reconstruction. In terms of practical politics, the constitutional crystallization of such a union might follow, rather than precede, the slow *ad hoc* development of a number of specific institutional arrangements performing a variety of functions.

In the light of the foregoing analysis, certain propositions dimly emerge: (1) A universal federation, in any approximate use of the term, is merely a distant dream. This does not rule out a universal "league." (2) The concept of European (regional) federation suggests the existence of greater politico-psychological obstacles than could be overcome within any reasonable period following the present war. (3) The idea of a Federal

Union of the Democracies, based at the outset on the participation of the United States and the members of the British Commonwealth, is intrinsically sound when tested by a number of the above principles.

No attempt has been made to examine the Streit or similar plans in terms of their relative desirability. Likewise, the feasibility of creation as well as of operation has been considered on a restricted rather than on a comprehensive basis. It is submitted, however, that the Streit proposal deserves a more careful analysis and evaluation at the hands of political scientists than it has hitherto received.

The state of the world in 1941 is sufficient excuse for a confessional postscript. I do not deny that the relationships between a limited democratic federation and the rest of the world must for a long time be based to a considerable extent on power— and the power of the federation must be made superior. I see no way to avoid that conclusion. In any ordered world, there must be power to maintain it. If that power cannot be generated from sources equally distributed all over the world, it must, and indeed will, be found somewhere. I should prefer that it arise from those people who, not because of any inherent racial qualities, but because of the state of their political development, are more likely than any other political group in the world today to exercise that power in a moral manner. The human world is made up of refractory, not plastic, materials. It cannot be made over in a day, or in decades. The demands of the machine age make the elimination of periodic war imperative; power is necessary (though not sufficient) to that end; and it is "we or they" who will wield that power. If the ultimate power be held by those societies in which moral and humanitarian forces are allowed to develop and operate unimpeded, therein lies the best chance (among present alternatives) for brutish power to be transmuted swiftly into "moral" power.

THE ATLANTIC CHARTER [4]

1. ORIGINS OF THE CHARTER

It would be contrary to the usual course of the international negotiations and agreements if we imagine that the Atlantic Charter sprang from Mr. Churchill's and Mr. Roosevelt's conversations as suddenly as Pallas Athene sprang forth "fully armed" from the head of her father, Zeus. Issues of the Charter had been discussed by Downing Street and the White House "since February," 1941, and the meeting might have taken place earlier had it not been for the campaigns in Greece and Crete. No record, however, was made public about the previous diplomatic negotiations, except that Mr. Roosevelt accepted the invitation to the meeting "late in July" and that the principal conclusion, known as the eight-point declaration and later baptized as the Atlantic Charter, was, in Mr. Roosevelt's words, "a joint idea" of both statesmen.

To consider the Charter as a diplomatic document of British-American action, we must connect it ideologically as well as politically with the peace movements and projects of both governments. As far as the American policy is concerned, the mission of Mr. Sumner Wells to Europe in February and March, 1940, probably had a very positive influence on Mr. Roosevelt's psychological development, since his "peace-feeler" learned in Berlin that the Nazis contemplate a settlement of the European affairs which will eliminate Britain and France from the European policy, thereby bringing Germany and America face to face. Addressing the governing board of the Pan American Union, on April 15, 1940, Mr. Roosevelt stated that their countries must have no illusions. Old dreams of universal empire are again rampant; there are races which claim the right of mastery, and they will encounter economic compulsions, shrewdly devised, to

[4] By Dr. Vlastimil Kybal, Minister from Czechoslovakia to Mexico at the time of the German invasion. *World Affairs Interpreter.* 12:367-81. January, 1942.

force great areas into political spheres of influence. At present, no nation is truly at peace if it lives under the shadow of coercion or invasion. Mr. Roosevelt condemned the "value of hate" as well as the "values of lies and cynicism," and declared that the path of peace will remain open to the American countries only if "we are prepared to meet force with force, if the challenge is ever made." In a similar way, in the special Defense Message of May, 1940, Mr. Roosevelt emphasized that the national ideal still was peace, but that the American people are ready not only to spend millions for defense but to give their services and even their lives for the maintenance of American liberties.

With a statesmanlike insight, Mr. Roosevelt became more and more aware of the fact that Nazism means not only a positive menace to American security, but also potential armed aggression, aimed at the form of government and at the kind of society that in the United States has been established for the American people, their own civilization, their religion, justice, and moral decency.

But it was only after the defeat of France that the element of security of the United States as an island-continent disappeared, and then the President determined to embark his country on a program of total defense, one part of which was the lease of naval and air bases in the North Atlantic and Atlantic-Caribbean zone, and the occupation of Greenland and Iceland; the second part pertaining to the huge rearmament of the national navy, land army, and air force; the third part aiming at all-out aid for Great Britain and other democracies. The President has said: "The whole program of aid for the democracies has been based on hard-headed concern for our own security and for the kind of safe and civilized world in which we wish to live." It is the "hard-headed concern" for American security which is the political and psychological basis of the Atlantic Charter and only from which its diplomatic value is to be measured and interpreted.

Regarding Great Britain, the common platform was created by two brutal facts, or to-be-facts, which with the defeat of France Hitler's world policy put into the heads of the responsible British and American leaders. These were that the British Navy is in peril and that the United States is in danger. As an attempt to invade England was expected "at any moment" at the beginning of 1941, Mr. Roosevelt sent his friend Mr. Harry Hopkins to London, as his personal representative, in order to talk with "old friends." Thus, the President would be able to maintain "personal contacts" with Great Britain. Later Mr. Willkie went to England with a personal letter to Mr. Churchill, and still later Mr. Winant as Ambassador and Mr. Harriman at the Embassy were to expedite the defense program, which the United States government has outlined as an "arsenal of democracy," with the object of defeating the dictatorships, in order to "continue to play its great part in the period of world reconstruction for the good of humanity." "Never in all our history have Americans faced a job so well worthwhile," Mr. Roosevelt disclosed, showing his full understanding of the responsibility of his country to humanity.

In Mr. Churchill's mind the cooperation between the United States and the British Empire in the task of extirpating the spirit and regime of totalitarian intolerance was a matter of absolute necessity. If this cooperation were to fail, he publicly stated, the British Empire, "rugged and embattled," might, indeed, hew its way through and preserve the life and strength of England and the Empire for the inevitable renewal of the conflict on worse terms after an uneasy truce. But the chance of setting the march of mankind clearly and surely along the highroads of human progress would be lost and might never return. "Therefore," Mr. Churchill declared, "we stand, all of us, upon the watch towers of history, and there is offered to us the glory of making the supreme sacrifices and exertions needed by a cause which it may not be irreverent to call sublime." Mr. Churchill considered as a most fortunate occurrence of world affairs that at the head of the American Republic should stand Mr. Roosevelt, a sincere and undoubted champion of justice and freedom and of the victims of wrongdoings wherever they may dwell.

The mutual esteem and confidence which existed between Mr. Churchill and Mr. Roosevelt and which were best expressed by Churchill's reply to Longfellow's verses, saying: "Put your confidence in us, give us your faith and your blessing, and, under Providence, all will be well," were very positively strengthened by Mr. Roosevelt's signature of the Lease-Lend Bill, "that monument of generous and far-seeing statesmanship, a new Magna Carta inspiring act of faith," as it was called by the British Prime Minister.

Bearing in mind these psychological manifestations, we do not need to seek for their translation into diplomatic acts and negotiations. The Atlantic Charter was certainly framed first in the minds of both leaders of the English-speaking world, and particularly in their firm determination that all resources and all power of their countries should be used in order to block the dictators in their march toward domination of the world.

In this determination they were upheld by the confidence shown them not only by the heads of the British Dominions, such as General Smuts, invoking the American "effective common authority" as the "key that opens the door through which the world can escape from chaos and suffering," or by Mr. Menzies, Prime Minister of Australia, calling the British and American peoples "trustees of liberty," but also by the representatives of the subjugated European nations. At their meeting in London, on June 12, 1941, Mr. Churchill remembered "our American friends and helpers drawing ever closer in their might across the ocean," and the idea of the "enduring peace," adopted by the assembly, undoubtedly was closely associated with the general peace policy of both Atlantic democracies.

Hitler's "treacherous" attack upon Soviet Russia was the last prelude to the Atlantic symposium. To the American government, the attack revealed the German plan for universal conquest, for the cruel and brutal enslavement of all peoples, and for the ultimate destruction of the remaining free democracies. Therefore, the Russian war was considered by "realistic" America as a danger to her own national defense and to the security of the New World. Consequently, in the opinion of the Washington government,

any defense against Hitlerism, any rallying of the forces opposing Hitlerism, from whatever source these forces may spring, will hasten the eventual downfall of the present German leaders, and will therefore redound to the benefit of our own defense and security. Hitler's armies are today the chief dangers of the Americas (statement by Acting Secretary of State Welles, June 23, 1941).

The same concept of the German danger for the whole British Empire as well as for the United States inspired the dramatic and bellicose speech of June 22, 1941, in which Mr. Churchill solemnly declared the British resolve "to destroy Hitler and every vestige of his Nazi regime." This resolve was materially evidenced by the military agreement signed in Moscow on July 13, and which involved not only the military aid, but also the diplomatic pledge not to negotiate with the enemy during the war any armistice or conclude peace except by mutual agreement.

The stubborn and surprising resistance of the Russian army and people against the German invasion, provoking the enthusiasm of the Slavonic nations, promoted Churchill's plans of preparing a general offensive against Nazi Germany as well as Mr. Welles' idea of "rallying of the forces opposing Hitlerism." At the foundation of these plans, however, lay, in the first place, the diplomatic, industrial, and military British-American cooperation. It was therefore necessary that the heads of both countries meet and through personal and technical discussion and consultation outline the program of common war and peace policy. That was the motive and the object of the Atlantic Conference, held on August 9 and 10 "at sea," and of the only public agreement, which issued from several conferences, known as the Atlantic Charter.

II. ANALYSIS OF THE CHARTER

The Atlantic Charter is not a peace and war program of the United States and British governments. It is only a statement of basic principles and fundamental ideas and policies regarding the establishment and the defense of "our type of civilization" in opposition to the Nazi system, which is largely based, according to Mr. Hull, on "barbarism and savagery." As Mr. Churchill more explicitly remarked, in his speeches on August 24 and September 9, 1941, those principles do not formulate peace or war aims, for which the time is not yet ripe, because the end of the war cannot yet be foreseen, but they represent only an open and full declaration of a common Anglo-American policy with which the subjugated nations have to associate themselves in order to achieve their long and painful liberating plans.

The first principle of the common Anglo-American policy is that *neither Great Britain nor the United States seeks any territorial gains or any other aggrandizement.* This is the basic principle of the security and good-neighbor policy which is adopted by both English-speaking countries. In general, this policy means, in practical application, that no other state should have to strive for conquest, and consequently Germany and other countries must give up all their conquests.

In this direction, in virtue of the Polish-Soviet Agreement, of July 30, 1941, Russia gave up its conquest of the Polish territory. What was the British attitude in this delicate affair? Great Britain assured them that the British did not recognize any territorial changes which have been effected in Poland since August, 1939. Nevertheless, as Mr. Eden mentioned in the House of Commons, no guarantee of frontiers in Eastern Europe will be undertaken by the British government. Consequently, the existing guarantee given to Poland through the Agreement between the

United Kingdom and Poland, of August 25, 1939, would no longer seem to hold good.[5] The same point of view was expressed by the American Undersecretary of State, Mr. Sumner Welles, who on July 31, 1941, declared:

> The United States does not recognize any change in Poland's status as a free, sovereign and independent nation. That position is maintained and continued. The Russian-Polish Agreement is in line with the United States policy of non-recognition of territory taken by conquest.

It seems, therefore, that the first common principle in the British-American policy underlines (1) the abandonment of the conquest and aggression policy by the signatory powers, in strict opposition to the German *Lebensraum* policy, and (2) the non-recognition policy with reference to other powers, without, however, containing any specific guarantees of frontiers.

In harmony with the same discernment, the second principle expresses the wish that *there be no territorial changes which would not conform to the freely expressed desires of the involved nations.* This principle, in connection with the third principle, condemns interventionist policies of all kinds, and it seems to include the principle of plebiscite and its eventual application to the solution of the territorial problems.

However, the governing fact of this principle is not the "territorial changes," but the condemnation of the "armed aggression." This idea is contained in Mr. Roosevelt's broadcast of July 18, 1941, as well as in Mr. Eden's Coventry speech, when he said that the plain meaning of the Roosevelt-Churchill Declaration is that no nation must ever be in a position to wage aggressive war against her neighbors.[6] Positively, the governing fact

[5] Cf. *The Times,* July 31, 1941, p. 5. The same point of view is admitted by the Poles. Cf. article by Mr. Stanislav Stronski, Minister of Information, "Alliance and Recognition of Frontiers," published in *The Polish Review,* September 15, 1941: "We have agreements for the recognition of frontiers and for mutual help against aggression. And it is these agreements that constitute a guarantee of our frontiers. No other guarantees exist."

[6] *The Bulletin of International News,* 1941, p. 1,138 (speech at Coventry, on August 30, 1941). Mr. Eden emphasized also that the Charter excluded all idea of hegemony or of zones of leadership in the East or the West, because the postwar world would require the collaboration of all.

is the Anglo-American policy of the liberation of the nations
from the Nazi yoke, as Mr. Churchill stated in the House of
Commons very clearly on September 9, 1941:

> We had in mind *primarily* restoration of the sovereignty, self-
> government and national life of the states and nations of Europe now
> under the Nazi yoke, and the principles which would govern any altera-
> tions in the territorial boundaries of countries which may have to be
> made.

In other words, any territorial change of the sovereign nations as far as it is realized by the aggression or conquest is
condemned. Territorial change or substitution of one sovereignty
by another must be carried on in accordance with the freely
expressed wishes of the peoples concerned, provided that all the
"peoples" of the respective country, not only the minority, freely
express their wish to change their state allegiance.

On the other hand, while rejecting the foreign armed intervention in the territorial settlement, the American and British
policy seems to maintain the possibility of changing the territorial
status quo by means of *peaceful adjustments,* thus preserving a
durable peace. In the same direction, Mr. Sumner Welles, in his
speech on the Restoration of Order, on July 22, 1941, emphasized
the fact that not only did the League of Nations die because of
the selfishness of the Americans, but also because it served as a
means of maintaining the *status quo* and not as a means of
"peaceful and equitable adjustments" between nations. The new
League of Nations must follow a policy the prerequisites of
which are abolition of offensive armaments, reduction of defensive armaments, and equal economic enjoyment. The Atlantic
Charter omits any mention of the League of Nations for obvious
political reasons as well as for unwillingness to define the principles in a concrete way, which is the general feature of this
document. Nevertheless, it contains the idea of respecting the
will of the people in case of territorial *resettlement,* probably
under the control of a supranational organization in order to

preserve the postwar political system which should avoid any war of conquest and any armed intervention among nations.

The same respect of the rights of man is expressed in the third principle. The American President and the Prime Minister of the government in the United Kingdom *respect the right of all peoples to choose the form of government under which they shall live; and they wish to see sovereign rights and self-government restored to those who have been forcibly deprived of them.*

In the writer's view, the statement contained in the first sentence of the Point is subordinated to the principle or rule clearly and positively expressed in the second part of the Standard. Moreover, according to the writer's opinion, the right of all peoples to choose the "form of government" they wish to have is not to be identified with the full right of self-determination which may lead to the separation of racial groups from their historical state. The right to choose freely their form of government cannot, in due logic, come into collision with the right of the restoration to the sovereignty of those peoples who have been forcibly deprived of it, while it concerns mainly the inner form of government under which they wish to live.

For instance, in a restored Austria the people will be free to choose the republican or monarchical form of government, and they cannot be forced to live under a totalitarian form of government imposed by the foreign country. In a restored Czechoslovak Republic the right of the national minorities will be fully respected, but it cannot oppose the fundamental right of this state to see restored its sovereign rights of which it has been forcibly deprived by Nazi Germany. If the Sudeten Germans or other racial groups wish to enjoy their own government, they should be free to do so, separating themselves from the Czechoslovak state and moving to another country.

As *The Times,* commenting on the Common Principles (August 18, 1941), observed, the fixing of frontiers is no longer, as it has been in the past, the most urgent or the vital part of peace making. The important thing now is not so much to change the location of frontiers but to change their character. In the same way *The Economist* (September 6, 1941), made the following pertinent observation:

The world between wars has seen that, not minorities only, but even majorities need safeguarding in their rights. A "majorities treaty" for Europe, or, to use the older phrase, a declaration that the rights of man are the concern of the international community, would state one of the necessary limitations upon the undefined "full sovereignty" that the Charter guarantees to each independent nation. Such a clause would at the same time place a salutary limit to the right of people to choose their own government. It should not be possible for a people to choose a Hitler any more than it is considered lawful for a man to commit suicide—or murder.[7]

At any rate, the form of government cannot be imposed upon a nation by a foreign country, since a choice is the sovereign right of all peoples.

The fourth principle refers to the *insuring to all states of access, on equal terms, to the trade and the raw materials of the world which are needed for their economic prosperity.* It expresses the American principle of free trade, the application of which would make impossible barter deals of the Nazi type. The main significance of this principle lies, however, probably in the fact that the two most powerful economic powers of the world show the "endeavor" to renounce to a certain degree their monopolistic holding of most of the world's raw

[7] In the House of Commons, on September 9, 1941, Mr. Churchill made plain that the promise of *full sovereignty* for the peoples of the world did not alter the government's policy within the British Commonwealth itself, *The Economist,* September 13, 1941.

In Mr. Roosevelt's speeches the "form of government" generally means the inner form of government, close to the "kind of society that we in the United States have chosen and established for ourselves," address to the Democratic Convention at Chicago, July 18, 1940, *The Bulletin of International News,* 1940, p. 935. In the President's mind the right of all peoples to choose the form of government is identified with the "freedom from fear, of being bombed or attacked by another nation," Five Freedoms' Speech, July 5, 1940, *ibid.,* p. 913.

At the Second Allies Conference in London, on September 24, 1941, the representative of the U.S.S.R. stated that the Soviet Union has applied, and will apply, in its foreign policy the principle of respect for the sovereign rights of peoples. Accordingly, the Soviet Union defends the right of every nation to the independence and territorial integrity of its country, and its right to establish such a social order and to choose such a form of government as it deems opportune and necessary for the better promotion of its economic and cultural prosperity. Cf. *The Inter-Allied Review,* October 15, 1941.

materials on which their privileged position and sometimes their economic imperialism were based, and new paths to a freer world economy based upon free competition were opened. However, the intent of both great powers is limited by the *"due respect for their existing obligations."* Moreover, the English-speaking powers do not renounce the possession which they have of the raw materials, but only wish to further the "enjoyment" of raw materials by all states, great or small, victor or vanquished, on equal terms. Consequently, neither the return of German colonies nor the eventual transformation of the colonial status into collective mandates is suggested or hinted by this principle.

The governing idea of the Economic Charter is freedom from want, through an international cooperation, just as the freedom from fear should be, in the political field, the essential condition of a durable and just peace. From this point of view, the first step is the elimination of restrictions on foreign trade and the suppression of monopoly of raw materials. The clause regarding the existing obligations, such as the Ottawa Agreements, was protested by The National Foreign Trade Council as not in accord with the general aim of the American trade policy as well as by the Foreign Minister of The Netherlands at the second Inter-Allied Conference in London.[8] Obviously the clause cannot be perpetuated without impairing the operation of the general rule.

Nevertheless, the aim in point four is positive as well as negative. It expresses the American principle of equality of opportunity for all and particularly Mr. Hull's five peace principles, enunciated on May 18, 1941. It also seems to imply Mr.

[8] *The Inter-Allied Review,* October 15, 1941. The Czechoslovak government added to the economic part of the Charter the following suggestion: "that within the future economic structure of the world small nations, like Czechoslovakia, by access to an equitable share of raw materials and other necessary help, must be given an opportunity as equal among equals *in close cooperation with their neighbors* to reconstruct quickly and permanently their devastated economic life," *ibid*.

To the political part of the Charter the same government made the observation that "even when total disarmament of the aggressor states is accomplished, the defensive positions of nations who, for a long time, have been victims of aggression will have to be considered," *ibid*.

Bevin's idea of equitable *distribution* of raw materials and basic foodstuffs *by cooperative action.*

In his speech at Llanduno, reported by *The Times,* on August 23, 1941, Mr. Bevin stated that the marketing of raw materials and of certain primary goods could no longer be left subject to the scramble of speculation; it must be organized. For his part he would like to pool goods on an international basis, pool the freights, and make a charge for their use on an international control. He hoped that the Declaration meant not only free access to raw materials but the working out of a system whereby these great basic materials would be free to mankind on equal terms.

Some of the principles regarding the reprovisioning of Europe and the establishment of a bureau in London were set forth at the second Inter-Allied Conference on September 24, 1941. The six-point Resolution adopted by the Conference can also be rightly considered as the first application of the fifth point of the Atlantic Charter.

In fact, the fifth point expresses the British and American *desire to bring about the fullest collaboration between all nations in the economic field with the object of securing, for all, improved labor standards, economic advancement, and social security.*

The policy of fullest economic collaboration eliminates any vindictive peace to be applied by the victorious Allies to the totalitarian powers as far as the world can be insured against the repetition of the war at their hands. Obviously, the condition of the fullest international collaboration in the economic field is the final destruction of Nazi tyranny, and the ensuing establishment of the kind of peace which would afford to all nations safety and freedom from fear and want. This means— and this is the political significance of the sixth principle of the Charter—that Great Britain and the United States jointly assume the responsibility both for *the destruction of Nazi tyranny* and Nazi domination over the German and other nations and *for the peace, security, and prosperity of the postwar world by means of a joint economic and military force.*

From a negative point of view, the principles of the fullest economic collaboration and of the organization of a safe peace after the destruction of Hitlerite Germany signify that the United States will abandon her isolationism, which, on the other hand, would bring her an increased prestige and prosperity in a free and safe world. Nevertheless, Mr. Roosevelt and Mr. Churchill established this policy only as a possibility, the realization of which they hope for. It will depend on other nations as well as their own to follow the example of the leaders of both democracies.[9] It will depend also on the well-balanced and really democratic policy, both economic and social, of all nations.

The seventh principle contains a common declaration of absolute *liberty of the seas.* This was declared in harmony with American policy, particularly with Wilson's peace terms (point one), and in opposition to Nazi submarine piracy which was encroaching upon such freedom. This principle is formulated as part of an integral peace organization which would serve international trade and which would be implemented by a sufficient international power. As far as concerns the British Empire, freedom of the seas signifies for all the Dominions freedom from fear, if the phrase can be taken to mean the restoration and maintenance of a *Pax Oceanica.* This peace, however, can be maintained only by the united action of the British Empire and the United States. Consequently, Great Britain, the United States, and the Dominions depend, each in similar measure, upon the efforts of all others (*The Times,* October 3, 1941).

The eighth and last point declares the main postulate of a peace reconstruction for the world by stating that the two signa-

[9] According to the report from Washington, published by *The Times,* August 22, 1941, Mr. Roosevelt described the Joint Declaration as so clear that it is difficult to oppose it in any major particular without automatically admitting willingness to accept a compromise with Nazism or to agree to a world peace which would give Nazism domination over large numbers of conquered nations and would permit Nazism after an armed interval to extend its control over Europe and Asia to the American Hemisphere.

tories believe that *all the nations of the world, for realistic as well as spiritual reasons, must come to the abandonment of the use of force. Since no future peace can be maintained if land, sea, or air armaments continue to be employed by nations which threaten, or may threaten, aggression outside their frontiers, they believe, pending the establishment of a wider and permanent system of general security, that the disarmament of such nations is essential. That will lead also the peace-loving peoples to the reduction of armaments.*

Practically, such a postulate demands that Nazi Germany be disarmed, as well as Italy and also Japan. The question of how this may be realized is not indicated. What seems to be certain is that the disarmament must be unilateral, being limited to the present and future aggressors, and that it will be carried out by the common action of the nations concerned.

Hitlerite Germany must be not only disarmed but destroyed, because only *"after the final destruction of Nazi tyranny"* can a safe peace be insured to all nations, including the German people. In the Charter there is no mention of the Fascist or other tyranny. However, the disarmament of the aggressors should be unilateral only until a wider and permanent system of general security is established. The permanent system of general security—political, social, and military as well—can be established only within the durable framework of international cooperation of both great and small, victors and vanquished nations.

While the question of the final peace settlement is left wide open by the authors of the Charter, the solution of the German problem was discussed with great frankness and eagerness. As Mr. Eden stated, the best way toward destruction of Nazi tyranny would be Hitler's deposition by the German people. When the Germans have provided themselves with a government with which it is possible to treat, Germany would be penalized in the military sphere, but encouraged in the sphere of economics. The military terms would include such provisions

as shall guarantee to the world that it is no longer in Germany's
power, another twenty years hence, to plunge mankind into
horrors of still another total war. Not only German war material but the "war potential"—that is to say, heavy industry
and vital raw materials—would be removed from Germany.

As *The Times* commented on August 18, 1941:

> It would seem that some system of pooled and centralized control
> not merely of armaments but of "war potential" at any rate over certain
> areas of the world, will ultimately be essential if the abandonment of
> the use of force which the Declaration rightly seeks is to be achieved.

Mr. Eden added:

> But essential security having been imposed, no thought of aggrandize-
> ment or revenge is entertained in this country. On the contrary, it is our
> practical interest to further the economic as well as the moral rehabilita-
> tion of Germany, because a starving and a bankrupt Germany in the
> midst of Europe would poison all of us who are her neighbors.

For the purpose of disarming Germany there must be created
an International Police Force, whose three essential stages were
pointed out by *"The Economist,"* September 6, 1941, as follows:
(1) the unilateral armament of Britain, America, and Russia
at the armistice; (2) the expansion within this nucleus of the
role already played by the Allied armies, French, Poles, Czechs;
and, finally, (3) the association with it of units from the former
aggressor nations. The system will not work if this last step
toward international cooperation is abandoned.

At any rate, both basic problems of the world peace—that is,
the disarmament of the aggressor states and the economic reconstruction of the world—presuppose the Anglo-American cooperation in the military, diplomatic, and economic fields. The
Atlantic Charter is a starting point or "a foretaste" of this cooperation between the two great powers in the rebuilding of a
peaceful world. Although the Charter represents the President's
standards, without binding Congress (Mr. Roosevelt sent the
text to the Congress "for information and for the record"), it

contains principles of the American official policy at the present time which are common with the British policy and the United States and Great Britain are therefore able to coordinate their efforts aiming at the establishment of world peace and world welfare.

As Mr. Roosevelt declared, the United States is going to play its full part as the arsenal of democracy and, when the dictatorships disintegrate, this country must continue to play its great part in the period of world reconstruction for the good of humanity. The Atlantic Charter shows the way to the American action: negatively, refusing any compromise with Nazism and, positively, stating basic ideas and policies which are common to the British policy and universal in their practical application.

They would also try to gain the confidence of the German people for the new world order which would be built by the Anglo-Saxon powers and by Russia with all the means at their disposal after the destruction of Nazi tyranny.

But the Charter is directed, above all, to the subjugated nations of Europe, to give them hope and assurance of an Allied victory and to align them for an offensive which would come at an opportune moment. It is a psychological as well as a political fact that in Mr. Churchill's and Mr. Roosevelt's minds, too, the common goal of their policy is indissolubly united with the liberation of the European nations from Nazi tyranny.[10]

[10] Cf. Mr. Churchill's Message broadcast, August 24, 1941, *The New York Times*, August 25, 1941: "Above all it is necessary to give hope and assurance of final victory to those many scores of millions of men and women who are battling for life and freedom or who have already bent down under the Nazi yoke."

Regarding Mr. Roosevelt's attitude, it was reported from Washington by *The Times*, August 18, 1941, that the President spoke with deep earnestness of one aspect of affairs which had been overlooked both in the Joint Declaration and in comment upon it. This was the need for an exchange of views on what was happening in the nations which are now living under Nazi subjugation. The more it was examined, he said, the more terrible it seemed that such influences should be at work in the conquered and affiliated nations. It was something which should be driven home more and more into the minds of the peoples of democratic lands.

Already in his address of March 16, 1940, Mr. Roosevelt stated that "it cannot be a sound peace if small nations live in fear of powerful neighbors, and that it cannot be a moral peace if freedom from invasion is denied to the small nations." *The Bulletin of International News*, 1940, p. 396.

This liberation has to be carried out not only by means of a military offensive of the Allies but also by a moral offensive of all the subjugated nations without excluding the German people themselves. For this purpose the British Prime Minister and the President of the United States formulated Eight Standards, which are common to the British and American democracies and which have to be accepted by the European and other nations until they are completely restored throughout the world.[11]

In conclusion, from the ideological and diplomatic point of view the Atlantic Charter is the solemn reassurance, by two world powers, of the faith and action, supported by all civilized peoples, that the only true basis of enduring peace is, negatively, the final destruction of the Nazi tyranny and the disarmament of all aggressor states and, positively, the willing cooperation of free peoples in a world in which, relieved of the menace of aggression, all may enjoy economic and social security as well as freedom of worship and of speech.[12]

COMMENT ON THE EIGHT-POINT DECLARATION [13]

The Commission first notes, with much satisfaction, the extent to which the general objectives and purposes of the Eight Points coincide with those stated in its own Preliminary Report. Both assume, as a prerequisite step, "the final destruc-

[11] On November 4, 1941, a Joint Declaration was signed in New York announcing formation of an Economic Bloc of Poland, Czechoslovakia, Yugoslavia, and Greece, which will embrace a population of 100,000,000 and will be enlarged by Hungary, Rumania, and Bulgaria after Germany is defeated. In the Declaration the conviction is expressed that the postwar peace will bring to the peoples enjoyment of the four freedoms defined in the Roosevelt-Churchill Declaration; and that the projected Union will play an important part in the reconstruction of Europe, *The New York Times*, November 4, 1941.

[12] The principles of freedom of religion and speech are not expressly incorporated in the Charter. However, Mr. Roosevelt, as author of the Four Freedoms' program, sending the Charter to the Congress, pointed out that "the Declaration of principles includes of necessity the world need for freedom of religion and freedom of information. No society of the world organized under the announced principles could survive without these freedoms which are a part of the whole freedom for which we strive," *The Department of State Bulletin*, August 23, 1941.

[13] By the Commission To Study the Organization of Peace. New York. p. 3-15. December, 1941.

tion of the Nazi tyranny." As the Commission Report puts it, in a prefatory note, "if these forces should fail (the forces that make for international justice) there will be no community of nations to organize." It accepts as the basis of thought in this field the interdependence of nations in the present day world, and agrees thoroughly with these two statesmen as to The World We Want—a world in which international cooperation shall prevail, rather than aggrandizement and conquest; a world in which the nation state remains the primary unit of international society, each free to choose its own form of government, but all bound to respect the rights of others in the community; a world in which, quoting from the Report, "human intelligence will organize and distribute the ample resources of nature so that all can live abundantly; a world in which intelligence will be devoted to human progress rather than destruction; a world in which a man's labor may be directed toward his own advancement."

The central theme of hope the world over, for the post-war period, is a new deal for the individual human being. In this respect, the situation differs from previous peace settlements, which were considered in terms of sovereign states. Most of the discussions now under way concerning post-war reconstruction recognize this attitude. All reports from England indicate a steady fusing of opinion in favor of a better life for the "little man." President Roosevelt's "freedom from fear and freedom from want," show that American leaders are also thinking in these terms. The key to thinking today is social justice, and the preoccupation of these two statesmen with this need is manifest in the Eight Points.

As to these principles and purposes, the Commission is happy to find itself in agreement with the Atlantic Charter. Its own Report goes much further, but the omission from the Eight Points of certain of the things sought by the Commission does not exclude them from future consideration. The leader of a democracy must rely upon the wishes of his people; and

the Commission believes that the American people are now
prepared to develop and implement the program laid before
them for their consideration. No more important duty rests
upon the American citizen today than the study of these
proposals.

Point 1. This, it is believed, represents fairly the sincere
belief of the American people. It states simply and squarely
the fundamental difference between the Axis Powers, which do
seek "aggrandizement, territorial or otherwise," and the United
States and Britain, who do not. It gives hope to the subjugated
peoples, and it would likewise give hope to the German people
in defeat. But it lays upon the American people a responsibility; it calls for a willingness to make concessions. If the
community of nations has now advanced to the stage in which
it denies to its members the methods of force by which some
of our great power and resources were acquired, we, as well
as others, will have to make concessions to those people who
do not have all they need; we cannot forbid the use of aggrandizement as a means of remedying an unfair situation unless we are willing ourselves to help with a remedy. It is not
merely an inexpensive self-abnegation which will impress them,
but real cooperation.

Point 1, however, should not be interpreted as an effort
to maintain a *status quo ante.* It may be necessary to make territorial readjustments, in order to lay a better foundation for
the international organization which will be needed if cooperation is to be substituted for aggrandizement. Nor should
it be interpreted so as to interfere with the responsibility for
maintaining order in the world which will fall upon the
victors, whether they like it or not. Such a control, of course,
should be temporary; it may be noted, however, that unless
a permanent world order is established, it might be necessary,
as Secretary Knox suggested, for England and America to
police the seas for a hundred years; it might even be necessary

for them to seize certain strategic points for their own protection against the range of modern war. The surrender of the right of conquest implies the substitution, therefore, of community order and justice. The Report of the Commission emphasizes this alternative.

Point 2. The results of this statement are similar to those of Point 1, but some difficulties are to be noted. The negative form of statement is a recognition of the fact that a positive right of self-determination is impracticable. What is meant by the word "peoples"? Who is to determine the composition of that group which is to express its wishes freely? Is this point to be taken as an assurance to the German people that their pre-war frontiers will be restored? Suppose that it should be regarded as essential to the reconstruction and security of the international order that Germany be broken into smaller units, would this be prohibited by Point 2? Would it, indeed, be possible to build a workable world order, or even European order, upon the frontiers which have existed in the past? It might require coercion to induce one people to accept the frontiers wished by another people, or to maintain them after they were established. There are involved also questions of colonies and mandated territories, and the restoration to their proper homes of many thousands who have been dislocated by the Nazi regime. It is difficult to see how these problems could be handled except through an international authority having power to decide and to enforce.

The solution of the perennial territorial conflicts of Europe is rather to be found in provisions for freedom of economic intercourse across these frontiers. The example of the United States is useful here. The prohibition, in the American Constitution, of barriers to intercourse between the forty-eight states has made the location of frontiers of minor importance, and has made loyalty to the community as a whole of greater interest than local loyalty.

Point 3. In this statement, again, a noble principle is enunciated, but difficulties are to be found in putting it into practice. Who is to determine the composition of the groups which shall choose their own forms of government? And by whom is this right to be guaranteed? It would seem again to be necessary to establish an international authority with power to control; if such a power is used to guarantee a free election in such nations, would it not thereby be requiring some degree of democracy as a requisite to membership in the international organization? If so, other questions are raised. Is it practicable or possible to require that all states shall be democratic? Is it true that democracy is so final and correct a form of government that no other form should be tried? Would this be to stifle political progress?

In its Statement of Aims (June 7, 1941) the Commission said: "Democracy, by its very principles, must concede to each nation the form of government which its people desire": but this was made "subject to the assurance by law of standards of individual liberty within each nation, and subject to an international guarantee against aggression by any nation." Further, "We hold that an international Bill of Rights, with such guarantees, is an indispensable basis of our own peace and security." These somewhat novel ideas were the result of belief that, unless an international system could reach into each state and guarantee against its rulers a certain freedom of thought and expression, it would be possible for a dictator— as Hitler has done—to pervert his people into ways contrary to international law and order. Point 3 should not, then, be interpreted so as to leave to a nation, or to leaders therein, the possibility of jeopardizing the maintenance of order through an organized community of nations. There must be such an international system to determine who are the people who can choose their form of governments, to enforce their right to choose, to prevent dictators or outsiders from interfering with that right, and to prevent the exercise of that right from doing injury to other members of the community.

The phrase "sovereign rights" also calls for attention. Doubtless, the authors of the Eight Points were thinking only of the restoration of national independence; but the term has unfortunate connotations. It could mean that unrestricted national power which has in the past meant anarchy in the community of nations; and if this should be the meaning, Point 3 would be quite incompatible with subsequent points, the realization of which undoubtedly would call for some diminution of sovereign power. As to this, the Preliminary Report of the Commission speaks emphatically: "A sovereign state, at the present time, claims the power to judge its own controversies, to enforce its own conception of its rights, to increase its armaments without limit, to treat its own nationals as it sees fit, to regulate its economic life without regard to the effect of such regulations upon its neighbors. These attributes of sovereignty must be limited." The Report then lists, in five paragraphs, the limitations or renunciations of sovereignty which are necessary to achieve the new world toward which both it and the Eight Points look.

If there is to be any meaning to subsequent points, Point 3 must not be so interpreted as to put national sovereignty above law and order in the community of nations.

Point 4. This, and the next two points, are important and far-seeing; with the objectives which they seek the Commission is in the heartiest agreement. Point 4 is in itself a limitation upon sovereignty, and is so stated in the Commission Report: "Nations must recognize that their right to regulate economic activities is not unlimited. The world has become an economic unit; all nations must have access to its raw materials and its manufactured articles. The effort to divide the world into sixty economic compartments is one of the causes of war."

From the government of the United States, an important further exposition of this point was made by Under-Secretary Welles in a speech on October 7, 1941. The entire speech should be read, for it is as forceful a brief presentation as can be found. Only a short extract can be quoted here, and it refers directly to Point 4: "The basic conception is that your government is determined to move toward the creation of conditions under which restriction and unconscionable tariffs, preferences and discriminations are things of the past; under which no nation should seek to benefit itself at the expense of another; and under which destructive trade warfare shall be replaced by cooperation for the welfare of all nations." If the American people will accept the advice of these governmental leaders—and it should not be concealed that it represents an important change in American policy—one of the greatest obstacles to the building of a prosperous community of nations will have been removed.

Two remarks are to be made concerning this point. The exception as to "existing obligations" could be interpreted in such a way as to destroy the entire meaning of the sentence. If it means that we are to be tied down to the past, that no changes can be made in the old treaty structure, then the whole of the Eight Points become unrealizable. Much of the present conflict goes back to the fact that certain states have advantages; if these are to be treated as vested interests, explosions will follow. The German people—who might otherwise be encouraged to cease fighting through the refusal of discrimination found in the words "victor or vanquished"—would look with skepticism and distaste upon a democratic new order based upon maintenance of the vested rights of the democracies. Large readjustments in the field of economic nationalism, which ought not to be thought of as sacrifices, will be called for, and especially from the United States and England; if they excuse themselves upon the ground of "existing obligations," their sincerity will be doubted and their leadership questioned.

Point 4 can be little more than words unless an effective international authority is established to carry it through. The Preliminary Report of the Commission demands "international machinery with authority to regulate international communications and to deal with such problems as international commerce, finance, health, and labor standards." It is exactly in this field that the American people will be most reluctant to make changes, for these changes—such as accepting external limitations upon our tariff policy—will appear to them to be sacrifices. Actually, such changes will not mean loss, but gain; the past few years have demonstrated that the prosperity of each depends upon the prosperity of all.

Point 5. The last sentence above carries over into this point, for it recognizes the interdependence of nations which is the foundation of all thinking in this field; it recognizes that no state alone is able adequately to advance the welfare of its members. Indirectly, Points 4 and 5 state again the fundamental opposition to the Nazi regime, which does not think in terms of the advancement of the human being. The League of Nations was not given sufficient authority to enable it to contribute, through international action, to social justice within nations. The experience of the International Labor Organization reveals the possibilities of contributing to human welfare, but likewise shows that more than "collaboration" is needed.

The Report of the Commission over and over again emphasizes that the attainment of social justice requires international agreement and organization. The efforts of any one state alone may be frustrated by conditions outside that state. We must go beyond bilateral treaties, for the relationships within the community of nations are far more complex. The problem of assuring social justice is an ever-changing one, and calls for continuing organization to deal with it. In this point is the essence of the new order which needs to be offered by democracies in opposition to the new orders of Germany or Japan.

Point 6. The defeat of the Nazi regime is a prerequisite to any advance toward international order. It is sure, however, that there will be other aggressors in the future; and the general principle of collective action against any aggressor must be the foundation of the future world order. It is a principle thoroughly proven in human experience and accepted by all peoples. War, in its modern character, makes freedom from fear and want impossible. No nation can provide for the economic security of its members, or enable them to live the sort of life which they may wish, so long as war is possible. The mere threat of war, in its modern character, necessitates totalitarian government at the expense of democracy. Each nation must divert the energies of its citizens from the activities which they prefer, and order them into fields of work which they may dislike, for the purpose of destruction. No one state is capable of protecting its citizens against this menace; each must turn to the collective action of the community of nations for support. This means a strong international government, with the physical power to defeat any attempt at aggression. The Report of the Commission calls for "Adequate police forces, world-wide or regional, and world-wide economic sanctions, to prevent aggression and to support international covenants."

Point 7. This point has a value in the immediate situation, but is of minor importance in the permanent settlement because its realization depends upon the ability of the community of nations to bring war under control. It is war which interrupts freedom of movement upon the seas, and of traffic in general; and, as Eugene Staley says, a stoppage in traffic is one of the greatest possible disasters in this interdependent world. If war can be brought under control, there will not be much difficulty as to the freedom of the seas. It should be noted, too, that it is naval action which interferes with movement upon the seas, and that Britain and the United States are the great naval powers. The restrictions which might be implied in this article would therefore be largely addressed to the United States and Britain. If the larger problem of war could be solved, navies would disappear, and with them the difficulty of keeping the seas open.

There must, of course, be freedom of communications and transportation if nations are to rely upon each other for their needs, but this freedom must be limited and administered if it is to be workable. Without such international regulation, freedom could be abused, and, like restoration of national sovereignty, lead to international anarchy.

Point 8. It must be recognized that, whether they like it or not, the responsibility for maintaining order in the world for a period following the cessation of hostilities will rest upon the victors, and that it will be necessary for them to retain their armed strength until order has been restored. But assurance needs to be given that they will not always retain this superiority. Disarmament must be universal, and Point 8 justly asks that all nations come to the abandonment of the use of force. The reduction of the "staggering burden of armaments" is part of the liberation of man from fear of aggression, but, as this point indicates, and as the intensive efforts of the League of Nations proved, disarmament depends upon the larger problem of security. "Abandonment" is not a strong enough word; the "renunciation" of the Pact of Paris was not enough. Security calls for more than the wish—and Americans have been guilty of much wishful thinking recently; it calls for an international system strong enough to protect those states which have disarmed and to provide justice for them. By implication, Point 8 recognizes this, for it speaks of a "wider and permanent system of general security." The Commission, though it likewise offers no blueprint, does sketch the outlines of such a system, and attempts to make clear the fact—which democratic peoples must recognize—that the cheering ideals offered them in Points 4, 5 and 6 are impossible of realization except through some form of international government. The American people have tried to secure reduction of armaments, and in vain; from their experience they should now be prepared to believe that they must join with others of the community of nations in a collective guarantee of security before they can hope for diminution of the burden of armaments.

Point 8 puts the imagination to work as to the procedure of making the peace. Its connotation and context give some cause for believing that its authors were thinking in terms of the transition or armistice period, whereas in other points they were thinking of permanent objectives. There is no doubt, as was suggested above, that a victorious England and America would actually have this power and responsibility; it will probably be true, also, that no one else will be able to shoulder the responsibility. In any case, decisions should not be taken by embittered and perhaps vindictive victors; they should be taken in the name of the organized community of nations. Even the democratic allies of these two nations would look askance at an Anglo-American domination of the world. They should have a voice in the decisions to be taken, and we would want them to have a voice. On the other hand, the British and Americans do not seek domination, and would not like a situation which might offer apparent ground for such a charge. The only alternative, however, is some sort of international association formed before the armistice bugle sounds, and prepared to share in the task of making decisions. Even though the power of action will belong to England and America, they should act only through the organized community—a community organized at once, ready for use when the time comes.

* * *

One word, found in the 8th Point, deserves special consideration. It is unusual to find statesmen using such a word as "spiritual"; and its use by these two statesmen illuminates their own feelings as to the issues now at stake, and recognizes the character of the sentiments of their peoples. There is a widespread conviction that disregard for fundamental moral principles led to the present conflict, and that for its solution we must return to those principles. In his Christmas Message of 1939, Pope Pius XII said:

Fifth. But even better and more complete settlements will be imperfect and condemned to ultimate failure, if those who guide the destinies of peoples, and the peoples themselves, do not allow themselves to be penetrated more and more by that spirit from which alone can arise life, authority and obligation for the dead letter of articles in international agreements—by that spirit, namely, of intimate, acute responsibility that measures and weighs his human statutes according to the holy unshakable rules of Divine Law . . . by that universal love which is the compendium of and most comprehensive term for the Christian ideal, and therefore throws across also a bridge to those who have not the benefit of participating in our own Faith.

The American Council of the World Alliance for International Friendship through the Churches, in a statement of 1940, says:

There is an imperative need in this critical time for strong faith in the sovereignty of God and in the brotherhood of man and for a resolute determination to do our part in establishing a better international order. As the dark reality of war spreads over the world and we hasten our defenses against it, we appeal to Americans of all faiths and creeds to be calm and just, and to hold steadfastly to their basic belief in God, democracy and the right.

The Malvern Conference, in England in January of 1941, held that the two most vital demands concerning social reconstruction should be: "The restoration of man's economic activity to its proper place as the servant of his whole personal life, and the expression of his status in the natural world as a child of God for whom Christ died."

Such expressions are frequent today, and stand in stark contrast to the purposeful destruction of religious and moral principles by the Nazi system. With this outlook the Commission To Study the Organization of Peace is in agreement, and the initial words of its Preliminary Report should be repeated:

No system of laws and organization can be of value without the living faith and spirit behind and in it. No world organization can succeed without mutual confidence on the part of its members. Our problem is largely an ethical one; it involves recognition on the part of all peoples, large and small, strong and weak, of the rights of others; a willingness on the part of all to make sacrifices for the general good; a belief in the existence of a power in the world that makes for righteousness.

The Atlantic Charter appeals to the most powerful force in humanity, the spiritual forces; a program such as it sets forth cannot fail to win the support of all men. Its emphasis is properly upon such ideals, for machinery alone is not enough; such machinery must have behind it the power of popular support and the directive force of ideals. On the other hand, machinery is necessary to put these ideals into effect, and it must be made clear to the peoples of the world, and particularly to the American people, that their hopes can not be achieved unless they are willing to establish and uphold an international system. Such an international government should be regarded, as the machinery of the state is regarded, simply as an agency through which humanity seeks to accomplish its purposes. It is the duty of democratic peoples to translate these hopes of human advance into machinery and methods; and the American people particularly must realize that such a system can have little hope without their whole-hearted support and even their leadership.

IF WE OWN THE FUTURE [14]

My basic quarrel with Federal Union is that to the extent that it provides for a world centralism, it is thinking in terms of a deliberative rather than a functional authority. And this, I think, not only strips it of its utility for the future, but is even a misreading of the spirit of the American Founding Fathers, from whom Federal Union derives so much.

The American Constitution, with its emphasis upon separated powers, and with its conception of government as a sequence of legislation, execution, and construction, is a poor model for a world state which will have to tackle problems more difficult than any in modern history. The essence of government today is to be found in a fusion between the consultative, the technical, and the administrative. This is true even of American national government: the measure of our capacity to survive has been our

[14] From *Ideas for the Ice Age*, by Max Lerner, Professor of Political Science, Williams College. p. 76-9. Viking Press. New York. '41.

capacity to move away from our earlier Congressional government and our later government by judiciary, toward a newer executive and administrative process. What is true of the American national state must be even truer of the world centralism we are envisaging. It will have difficult problems to deal with— of the recognition and support of constitutional governments in the defeated countries, of the supplying of a devastated and famished Europe and Asia with the means of sustaining life and rebuilding industry, of the rebuilding and replanning of whole cities and areas, of the movement of industries and the repatriation of peoples, of international policing, of trade and colonies and foreign investments. And in this context the emphasis of Federal Union upon an international legislative assembly, with its membership carefully distributed among the constituent nations, is something short of realism. Our recent experience with Congress should have indicated the failure of parliamentary decision in the problems with which modern governments are chiefly concerned.

I have said that the essence of modern government lies in a fusion of the consultative, the technical, and the administrative. An application of that principle to the world federal state would mean that the tasks I have described would have to be accomplished not in the forum of a world assembly, but by mixed commissions including political representatives of particular class and functional outlooks, technical advisers in the economic, military, labor, educational areas, and competent trained administrators. This would provide at once political power and responsibility, technical *expertise*, administrative realism. I should be willing to trade the entire proceedings of a world assembly for even a small portion of these.

Nor need these be mainly paper constructs. One of the heritages of the era of constitutional government has been a reliance on the power of words on paper to constitute a polity. Woodrow Wilson's League of Nations group suffered from the same itch for constitution-making, for the structural as contrasted with the organic. Less important than a ready-made constitution is the succession of steps from where we are now, through economic cooperation with Latin America, war cooperation with Britain, Russia, China, the setting-up of an economic general staff not only for the war effort but for the postwar effort as well, the transition from the present "phantom" governments of the vanquished states in London and the economic and military missions in London, Moscow, Washington, Chungking, to the mixed commissions I have been describing, the institutionalization of these makeshift arrangements until they become an organic part of the national governments concerned and therefore of the world state. A peace conference there will have to be; but we must not depend on it to take more than a few preliminary postwar steps. The creative work will have to be done outside the feverish atmosphere of a peace conference, vulnerable as it is to every pressure and intrigue.

That means that we shall have to envisage a transition period between the end of the war and the effective functioning of the new world economic arrangements and political mechanisms. In that transition period the nations that have the economic power, the political prestige, the moral strength in the world will have to take the pragmatic leadership. They will have to solve the enormously difficult problem of finding or setting up governments in the defeated countries with which they can deal, a problem serious enough in nations like France and Rumania, but almost insuperable in Germany itself. Ferrero has suggested, in his recent *Reconstruction of Europe,* that the European powers faced the same problem after the Napoleonic wars, and that it was the genius of Talleyrand that found the solution. However that may be, the test we shall do best to use is not merely legitimacy in the line of pre-Hitler succession, but the extent to which the government has the confidence of the large majority of its people, the extent to which its members can point to genuine anti-fascist and pro-democratic behavior in the past, the extent to which they can combine firm and realistic action with strength enough to brook an opposition.

In all that I have said the accent has been on a pragmatic effectiveness within a democratic framework. That was, I think, the spirit of those who founded our government. They used the best wisdom of their time in an approach to the problems of their time. We cannot be content with reverting to their political forms in our approach to the problems of our time. It will be better for us to borrow their spirit than their solutions.

There remains the question of the auspices under which all this can be accomplished. That they must be democratic is a first principle. But one does violence to democracy by speaking of an "American century," or dreaming of a British-American condominium over the world. Democracy is a world force, capable of liberating still untapped productive and moral energies all over the world. A democratic postwar world would mean one which put into power in every nation, and at the world center, those groups that best understood and expressed the felt needs and the possibilities of their culture.

There has been a good deal of talk, and not all of it unjustified, of the gap between have and have-not nations. To move from the fact of possession to the fact of social function is as necessary in the international as in the national sphere. Similarly one can draw a parallel between the movement within a nation away from the manipulation and exploitation of scarcities to the fullest expansion of productive capacities, and the similar movement in the international sphere. The democracy of the future will mean the sort of national and world government which allows for these directions. And this must mean a transfer of governmental function to the groups which have the technical skill and the knowledge of the industrial and administrative arts, the groups that are untrammeled by the vested ideas that have not worked in the past and unblinded by disabilities of social vision, the groups which are willing to convert into general living standards and cultural potentialities the goods and services whose production they organize.

Without an effective transfer of social function and political power to these groups and their leaders, the present war against fascism will not finally have been settled.

THE WAR AND THE PEACE [15]

The search for a creative and an enduring peace demands a true understanding of the world situation and of the conditions which have brought it into being. The war is a reflection of a crisis in civilization itself. Its ultimate cause lies in the common failure to utilize and control in accordance with the principles of morality the powers and resources which the developments of science and machinery have made available in the modern world. It is upon the redemption of this failure that a valid peace depends. To separate, therefore, the issues raised by the war from those involved in the making of the peace is to misinterpret the character of the crisis. The essential problem is to find ways and means of moulding to desirable ends the revolutionary changes which are already in process and which are at once the nature and consequence of the war.

This task cannot be achieved without a moral inspiration and purpose. Democracy by definition proclaims the significance of the individual person, the right to a true freedom for all men, irrespective of race or nationality, and the reality of the common interest which unites them. But the democratic peoples have so far lacked the faith and the courage to implement these principles. They have only too frequently betrayed them in the ordering of their social and economic life, and so have produced the national disorders and the recourse to violence as the apparently sole hope of change which have imperilled civilization and have led to war. If the basic principles of democracy do indeed reflect a faith and a philosophy, they must be made to shape our aims and institutions as completely as the rival philosophies have found expression in their systems. There can be

[15] By Commission To Study the Organization of Peace. New York. Bulletin No. 8. p. 3-4. August 1941.

no driving force sufficient to establish a new social and international order unless it rests upon a deep sense of spiritual purpose, a clear vision of the goal and a courageous pursuit of the practical steps which its fulfilment requires.

The new international order which under this impulse we are to seek to achieve must, we believe, have three major features:

1. It must be based upon a common standard of social values —a new charter of human rights and obligations to be applied to all peoples irrespective of race or nationality, class or creed.

2. It must establish a new international economic authority (to be developed from existing agencies where these are serviceable) charged with the responsibility of raising the general standard of living and for this purpose of securing a more equitable distribution of raw materials to meet the primary needs of mankind. It must as a corollary liberate the peoples in colonial areas from exploitation and poverty.

3. It must create a system of political cooperation for the world community based upon far-reaching modifications of national sovereignty, and involving the setting up of an international authority having among other tasks the responsibility of effecting a progressive world disarmament and of controlling in the meantime such armaments as may remain.

If Great Britain and the British Dominions are to commend the conception of democratic freedom which they profess to serve and which they offer to the peoples of Europe and the wider world, this freedom must be demonstrated as a reality, not merely in Great Britain and the British Dominions, but also in the "dependent" areas which they control. In this relation the present situation in India is of vital importance. If a full settlement of the constitutional problem cannot be reached in the midst of war, it is none the less essential that we should prove our sincerity by prompt negotiation with Indian leaders in order to establish a transitional government and by a definitive acceptance of India's freedom at the close of the war.

The new international order envisaged in these proposals implies the realization of a better social and industrial order within each country. The problem of international economic cooperation is at root a national rather than an international problem. The modern industrial nation with its millions of undernourished people is unable to consume as rapidly as it can produce. The result is the feverish and provocative struggle for overseas markets and areas of influence, the building up of trade restrictions, and the creation of the economic frictions which lead to war. The problem originates in the social and industrial order at home and the key to its solution is to be found in the enhanced well-being of the mass of the people everywhere. It is essential, therefore, to promote a program of domestic social change which has as its central objectives:

1. A monetary system which makes finance and credit the servant and not the master of the community, and establishes the satisfaction of human need as the governing factor in production and distribution.

2. The effective social control of the land and other principal means of production—especially those which tend to be monopolistic.

3. The highest standard of life which the productive resources of the community make possible for all its citizens.

4. A system of education making full educational opportunity available to all members of the community.

COMPARATIVE TABLE OF PEACE AIMS AND PRINCIPLES [16]

Comparative table of the scope and direction of the aims and principles enunciated respectively in (1) the Atlantic Charter;

[16] By Bertram Pickard, former Chairman of the International Consultative Group, Geneva, Switzerland, and for fourteen years secretary of the Friends Center in that city. Commission To Study the Organization of Peace. New York. Bulletin No. 9. p. 1-3. September-November, 1941.

(2) the Fourteen Points of President Wilson; (3) The Pope's Five Peace Points; and (4) the proposals (six principles plus a suggestion regarding international organization) set forth in "A Call to Persons of Good Will" issued by the American Friends Service Committee in June 1941.

Aims and Principles	Atlantic Charter 8 Points	Wilson's 14 Points	Pope's 5 Points	A.F.S.C. 7 Points
POLITICAL				
Self-determination, national and cultural independence: equality of rights	2, 3, 6	6-13 [17]	1	3
Colonial policy	..	5	4 (implied)	6
Disarmament	8	4	2	1
General security through international institutions	8	14	3	1, 7 (implied)
Open diplomacy	..	1	..	..
Freedom of the seas	7	2	..	..
Protection of minorities ..	6 (implied)	..	4	..
ECONOMIC AND SOCIAL				
Removal of economic barriers (access to markets and raw materials) ...	4	3	4 (implied)	5
International economic cooperation for mutual prosperity and social security	5	..	4 [18] (implied)	4

[17] The essentially Wilsonian doctrine of self-determination, curiously enough is not included in the 14 Points as a general principle. But in his famous speech to Congress of January 8th, 1918, Wilson demanded that "the world be made safe for every peace-loving nation" in language which is clearly reflected in Point 3 of the Atlantic Charter and Point 1 of the Pope's 5 Points. Points 6-13 of the 14 Points represent specific applications of the principle of self-determination relating to the post-war situations of Russia, Belgium, France, Italy, Austria-Hungary, the Balkans, Turkey, and Poland.

[18] It should be noted that when the Pope's 5 Points were approved jointly by the leaders of the Catholic, Anglican and Free Churches in England in a joint

Aims and Principles	Atlantic Charter 8 Points	Wilson's 14 Points	Pope's 5 Points	A.F.S.C. 7 Points
Reduction of migration barriers	..	..	• 4 (implied)	5
JURIDICAL				
Peaceful change of status quo	..	..	3	2
ETHICAL AND RELIGIOUS				
Personal freedoms	6 [19]	..	..	.. [20]
Conformity to Christian ideal and laws of God	..	..	5	.. [21]

ROOSEVELT-CHURCHILL DECLARATION [22]

The President of the United States of America and the Prime Minister, Mr. Churchill, representing His Majesty's Government in the United Kingdom, being met together, deem it right to make known certain common principles in the national policies of their respective countries on which they base their hopes for a better future for the world.

1. Their countries seek no aggrandizement, territorial or other;

letter entitled "Foundations of Peace—a Christian Basis" which appeared in *The Times* of December 21st, 1940, 5 additional "standards" were added "by which economic situations and proposals may be tested." These are clearly concerned both with mutual prosperity and social security.

[19] It should be noted that the two-fold "freedom from fear and want" referred to in Point 6 of the Atlantic Charter was expanded by interpretation in President Roosevelt's Message to Congress of August 21st, to cover also "the world need for freedom of religion and freedom of information," thus including all the "four freedoms" to which the President has often referred in the past.

[20] Though no enumerated point stresses this, it is implied in the context of the statement notably in the plea for "the preservation of that unique human spirit out of which both democracy and all that is precious to civilization has sprung and has flourished."

[21] Again, though no enumerated point has the Christian emphasis of the Pope's Point 5, the whole context of the A.F.S.C. statement enforces that same basic insistence upon the relationship between true peace and the Will of God.

[22] The Atlantic Charter or Eight-Point Program agreed upon by Prime Minister Winston Churchill and President Franklin D. Roosevelt, August 14, 1941. *International Conciliation.* 372:595-6. September, 1941.

2. They desire to see no territorial changes that do not accord with the freely expressed wishes of the peoples concerned;

3. They respect the right of all peoples to choose the form of government under which they will live; and they wish to see sovereign rights and self-government restored to those who have been forcibly deprived of them;

4. They will endeavor, with due respect for their existing obligations, to further the enjoyment by all States, great or small, victor or vanquished, of access, on equal terms, to the trade and to the raw materials of the world which are needed for their economic prosperity;

5. They desire to bring about the fullest collaboration between all nations in the economic field with the object of securing, for all, improved labor standards, economic adjustment, and social security;

6. After the final destruction of the Nazi tyranny, they hope to see established a peace which will afford to all nations the means of dwelling in safety within their own boundaries, and which will afford assurance that all the men in all the lands may live out their lives in freedom from fear and want;

7. Such a peace should enable all men to traverse the high seas and oceans without hindrance;

8. They believe that all of the nations of the world, for realistic as well as spiritual reasons, must come to the abandonment of the use of force. Since no future peace can be maintained if land, sea or air armaments continue to be employed by nations which threaten, or may threaten, aggression outside of their frontiers, they believe, pending the establishment of a wider and permanent system of general security, that the disarmament of such nations is essential. They will likewise aid and encourage all other practicable measures which will lighten for peace-loving peoples the crushing burden of armaments.

FRANKLIN D. ROOSEVELT
WINSTON S. CHURCHILL

EXCERPTS

We strongly believe that education must deal with the future as well as with past and present problems; we therefore believe it is a major task of American colleges to give active consideration to the problem of post-war reconstruction and reconciliation, and to the development of plans for a world in which war will no longer be necessary.—*Point 6 of Resolutions adopted by faculty and students of Antioch College December 11, 1941. Antioch Notes. Ja. 15, '41. p. 8.*

The Atlantic Charter seems to guarantee that one of Britain's mistakes after the last war shall not recur. Great Britain and the U.S.A. have undertaken not to turn away from Europe, the moment arms are laid down; but to accept common responsibility for building up Europe in such a way as to make a third world war impossible in the near future.—*Fortnightly. N. '41. p. 419.*

The Anglo-American alliance for policing the post-war world, the avowed aim of the Charter of the Atlantic as interpreted by Prime Minister Churchill and Secretary Knox, promises not the elimination of the war system or imperialism, but an endless cycle of wars abroad and fascist regimentation at home to maintain them.

Only a democratic and socialist victory followed by a democratic and socialist peace can free the world from the recurrent fear of endless war.—*Statement by the National Executive Committee of the Socialist Party. Call. Ja. 3, '41. p. 1.*

For months already Nazi propagandists have been broadcasting from Germany attacks against the plan of Union Now— a significant attention for a foreign government to pay to a private campaign. The Nazis have been trying to alarm British listeners by telling them that Union means reducing Britain to the status of a 49th State in America. They have sought to turn Americans against Union by the lie that Union means handing America over to the British.

The fact that the Nazis have been trying so long to prevent Union by this old "Divide-and-Rule" game—that fact speaks for itself on the timeliness of our petition for Union Now.— *Clarence K. Streit, Author of "Union Now." Statement, D. 18, '41. mim.*

Consider the matter of waging war in association with other peoples against a common enemy. This may be done on the basis of an alliance of governments or it may be done as a union of peoples. The British and French started out with an alliance, and we saw its disintegration last summer, giving way to a separate peace on the part of France.

Churchill knows his American history. He recalled that the colonists fought George III, not on an alliance basis, but as a union. Even with the colony of New York occupied by the British, there was no question of a separate peace, because the powers to wage war and conclude peace were placed in the hands of the Continental Congress. New York fought on until victory was assured for all the colonies. With that experience in mind, Churchill offered France complete union at the eleventh hour. It came too late.

Are we not today faced with the same choice between alliance and union in our collaboration with the British democracies? Past experience should teach us that now, as then, in union there is strength, and that in alliance lurk myriad hazards.— *Thatcher M. Adams, Hamden, Conn. New York Times. My. 14, '41. p. 20.*

No amount of hindsight will enable us to undo the terrible errors of the past; but we can determine now never to repeat them. The airplane has made it forever impossible for us again to ignore any future threat to the peace of the world from any quarter whatever. Even the oceans have now been shown to be only partially protecting frontiers which must give less protection each year. We can no longer be indifferent when any great nation anywhere becomes the tool of a dictatorial, secretive and belligerent government. If peace is to be preserved, it must be preserved by nations known to be both strong enough and determined enough to stamp out any threat to peace before it has been allowed to grow to any real dimensions.

The United States and the British Commonwealth must form the democratic nucleus of such a group. They alone, in fact, acting together, would assure the success of such a group. The war is certain to be won, and the world's future civilization to be preserved, if the two great English-speaking peoples, in Mr. Churchill's magnificent words, learn to "walk together in majesty, in justice and in peace."—*Editorial "For Anglo-American Unity." New York Times. D. 27, '41. p. 18.*

Some day there shall be a union of all the peoples of the world in a universal brotherhood.

Some day the North and the South and the East and the West shall live together in happy comradeship.

But the time has not yet come for this.

The time *has* come for a mighty Indo-British Commonwealth of Free and Interdependent Nations.

The time *has* also come for a great alliance between this Commonwealth and the United States of America.

The time *has* also come for a United States of Europe.

And foreshadowing the union of the peoples of the world, the time *has* come for a worldwide fellowship of nations and of faiths.

The last great war should have begun its true peace in these.

Its purpose failed.

This still greater catastrophe must begin its true peace in these, or it too will have failed.

And then will come another war.

All servants of peace must help so to prepare public opinion in every land that nothing less than these shall satisfy the public will when the time comes for the war to end and for peace to begin.—*Conscience (India). O. 3, '40. Special Supp.*

The answer to enemy propagandists who pretend that the Atlantic Charter is merely a plan prepared by British and

American capitalists to dominate Europe is simple enough. There
is a world of difference between a free association of peoples
whose internal liberties and constitutions are scrupulously respected, and the forced cooperation imposed on conquered
peoples by conquerors who have violated not only their international obligations, but the most elementary rules of international law concerning occupied countries. There is the same
difference between the acceptance by independent states of an
international authority for defense and economic collaboration,
and the submission of oppressed countries to the authority of
one nation or one "race" to economic and military oppression.
But in order to bring home this argument to all and to vindicate
the principle of interdependence from the attacks directed against
it, it is essential that the distinctions made between the policy
pursued by the small peaceful powers, from 1919 to 1939, should
be considered in all fairness, and that responsibilities for former
mistakes should not be systematically shifted from the stronger
to the weaker shoulders. The spirit of the Charter is a spirit
of friendly cooperation, and friendly cooperation in the future
implies a friendly understanding of the past.—*Emile Cammaerts,
Professor of Belgian Studies and Institutions, University of London. Contemporary Review. Ja. '42. p. 20-1.*

The day is past when any nation can stand alone. The price
of liberty, as well as the price of international law and order, is
effective cooperation, with mutual sacrifices for the common
good.

Such cooperation does not necessarily mean a new and more
powerful League of Nations. It does not necessarily mean "union
now" in some form of federated world government. It could
conceivably mean nothing more complicated than extension of the
basic principle of the Monroe Doctrine to cover the British Commonwealth of Nations, with equivalent reciprocal guarantees for
our protection. This would place under control of peace-loving
democratic peoples three-fourths of the potential military power
of the entire world. The precise type of cooperation is less im-

portant than the fact of cooperation. But cooperation of some sort there must be. Only thus can overwhelming potential force be marshalled on the side of justice, and the security of all be assured at reasonable cost to each.—*Douglas Johnson, Professor of Physiography, Columbia University; member of American Commission To Negotiate Peace at Paris in 1918-19. International Conciliation. D. '41. p. 719.*

If the Declaration of the Atlantic, signed by the President of the United States and by the Prime Minister of the United Kingdom and released to the world on August 14, 1941, is taken merely as a restatement of the democratic faith in international relationships, nine-tenths of its significance will be lost. The ideas are not particularly new nor is the language unduly inspired. Its true significance lies in the identity of the signatories and in the place where it was signed. The Declaration marks, in effect, the assumption by the two great English-speaking democracies of the leadership of the free world. It serves notice that, when the victory has been won, the ideas that will be dominant in the world will be the faiths and the aspirations and the doctrines that are common to Britain and America. The fact that its only date line is "The Atlantic Ocean" is as significant as the signatories. Nothing could have more dramatically demonstrated the change that has come over the role of the Atlantic in the popular thinking of both countries. The ocean is no longer a barrier, a moat, a gap in space. It is a highway, a meeting-place, a common avenue of approach. Implicit in every line of the Declaration is the proclamation that hope for the world's future—the only hope—lies in the continued collaboration of the Oceanic Commonwealth of Free Nations.—*Geoffrey Crowther, Editor, The Economist, London. Foreign Affairs. O. '41. p. 1.*

The idea [of a federal democratic union] is an intriguing one, especially when considered in all its manifold implications. It would unite the 13,539,113 square miles of the British Empire with the 3,738,395 square miles of the United States, the combined territory exceeding that of the U.S.S.R. and China put together. The combined populations would total about 635,000,000 people, almost equal to the combined populations of the U.S.S.R. and China. The union would bring about ideal conditions in certain respects. Its citizens would be able to move to and between a large number of countries without the vexation of visas and customs formalities.

Politically, it would seem to be a comparatively simple matter to establish such a union, but the economic difficulties would be enormous. In the years after World War I, Britain had difficulty in holding her empire together. Politically and ideologically the various units of the empire were united, but economic rivalries represented a serious centrifugal force. Britain was compelled to grant Dominion status to Canada, South Africa, Australia and New Zealand—later to the Irish Free State—and to grant certain economic "preferences" to the Dominions in order to preserve their attachment to the mother country.

In a union embracing still more numerous lands and peoples the same difficulties would be encountered on a larger scale. That is why the idea of union, along the lines of Clarence Streit's plan, may forever remain a distant dream.—*China Weekly Review*. Je. 28, '41. *p*. 109-10.

The formal approval of the Atlantic Charter on Wednesday by the Allied governments at present domiciled in London and by the government of the Soviet Union is an event of considerable importance, for it means that the governments concerned have decided after full deliberation to accept unreservedly principles whose recognition may in some cases involve a definite change in national policies. Russia, for example, in abjuring all territorial aggrandizement, must be held to waive all claim to the Polish territory she has acquired since Poland was first invaded, while the Poles themselves must be a little concerned as to how far the inhabitants of some parts of their former territory now acquire the right of self-determination. Now that the application of the Atlantic Charter is being discussed as a practical proposition, as of course it should be, it is important to decide what its starting-point is. It must clearly provide for the restoration of the *status quo* existing some time earlier than the outbreak of the present war. The forcible annexation of Austria took place in March, 1938. That, emphatically, is a territorial change which must not stand unless it accords with the freely-expressed wishes of the Austrian people; which suggests that the aim must be a return to pre-1938 frontiers in Europe, subject to any changes consistent with the principles of the Atlantic Charter. No change achieved by force can be valid for that reason, but certain changes made by force may in spite of that be validated on other grounds. The Dutch Foreign Minister's demurrer to the "existing obligations" reservation in the clause dealing with equality of trade conditions and access to raw materials portends much future argument.—*Editorial. Spectator (London). S. 26, '41. p.298.*

The Atlantic Charter, drawn up by President Roosevelt and Prime Minister Churchill, indicates two possible lines of approach toward the German problem: unilateral disarmament of Germany during a period of reconstruction; and then efforts, in the long run, to provide Germany with free access to raw materials and other economic opportunities. The Charter provides for unilateral disarmament of Germany (exactly what was done in 1919), *"until such time as general conditions of peace have been established."* We may assume that during this period, whose duration remains indefinite, Britain and her allies would pool their military resources to form an international police force, which would be used to police Europe, and possibly other warring continents. At the same time, most Britishers appear to believe that during the period of receivership the Germans should be given an opportunity to develop, without outside compulsion, organs of self-government representative of the people, with whom the rest of the world could ultimately reach a peace

This future settlement, as indicated in the Atlantic Charter, would endeavor to provide for long-term reconstruction not only settlement.

of Europe, but of the world. It would seek to equalize the position of all countries with respect to raw materials, migration of populations and access to colonial territories, in an attempt to remove some of the most outspoken grievances of Germany, Italy and Japan. It would require, presumably, not only pledges of good conduct by Germany, Italy and Japan, but also concrete evidence of readiness on the part of Britain, the United States and the British Dominions to make economic and financial contributions for the common good. It would require, in addition, social reorganization in all countries to meet the needs of a new world order.—*Vera Micheles Dean. Research Director, Foreign Policy Association. "Struggle for World Order." Foreign Policy Assn. New York. p. 87-8.*

There is, of course, no conflict between the idea of the League and the idea of Federal Union. The one is only the extension of the other; and had it not been for the devoted labors of the League's supporters over the past twenty years there would be little enough hope for a United States of Europe today. Nor is it really the case that it would be more difficult to create a federation than a league; in some important respects it would be easier. But there are differences between the league idea and the federal idea. And it is by the study of these differences that we may be able to find the real cause of past failure and the true foundation for future success.

First of all, then, what do we mean by a Federal Union, and how does it differ from a League of Nations. Broadly speaking, a League of Nations is an association of sovereign states, each one of which maintains complete freedom of action for itself over the whole field of politics, subject only to such limitations as it may agree to be binding upon itself and other sovereign states. The unit of the League is the state, and the central authority of the League deals only with governments and not at all with peoples whom those governments represent.

In a Federal Union, on the other hand, the states which are constituent members do not have unlimited freedom of action over the whole field. In part of that field, normally foreign policy, defence policy and currency policy, they surrender their power to the federal authority; in the remainder they retain complete control. In purely domestic matters the federal government has no authority, but within the field of federation the state governments have none and the federal government is responsible not to the state governments but directly to the peoples themselves. A Federal Union, therefore, is an association not of governments but of peoples, and the unit is not the state but the citizen.—*Richard Law, Member of Parliament, Great Britain. "Federal Union and the League of Nations." p.1-2. n.d.*

I do not wish to be misunderstood. Something in the nature of an overriding International Police Force, under international control, will be indispensable when this war is over. It may be modelled on the present constitution of the Royal Air Force, with its Polish, Czechoslovak, Free French and other national formations within a comprehensive framework. We shall also need international organization and control of many aspects of economics and finance, industry and communications, and access to raw materials. In some directions restrictive or repressive measures may be required. Privileges may have to be withheld from the unworthy until they prove themselves worthy. Yet my vision of the future is colored by belief that the world cannot be lastingly improved by restraints alone, and that the ideal peace force must be so constituted that all peoples will be eager to join it for the honor and glory of human service. I have said that the American Lease-Lend Act is a revolutionary stroke of political genius. Free from belittling conditions it put the wealth and the material resources of the United States at the service of nations fighting for freedom. It made helpfulness in support of noble endeavor a new international law. Only through the extension of the spirit of this law to Europe and to the world can I see an opening into a better future, a future in which even the Germans may share when they have cast out the demon of militarism and have learned that the will and the power to do right are the only abiding sources of might. Without some such ideal as this to throw light upon our path the future may be troublous and dark. Beset by difficulty and hardship it must be. Yet there will be hope for mankind, beyond what might otherwise seem the Slough of Despond into which we shall enter when guns are silent and bombs rain no more from the skies, if, under inspired leadership such as the British Commonwealth, the United States and our Allies can provide, the nations are brought to see the refulgence of vital peace.—*Henry Wickham Steed, British Editor and Author. Contemporary Review. S. '41. p. 151.*

Point 2, we confess, fills us with misgiving. It states that the signatory Powers desire to see no territorial changes that do not accord with the freely expressed wishes of the people concerned. Shall Germany be allowed to keep Alsace-Lorraine? It may well be that by terrorism and deportations she has replaced the pro-French majority by a pro-German majority. If a ballot were to be held, the "wishes of the people concerned" would express themselves for Germany and against France. We have no doubt at all that neither President Roosevelt nor Mr. Churchill have any desire to see Germany confirmed in any of her conquests, but in politics it is always dangerous to enunciate general principles, especially when their practical application may produce results that are the opposite of what their authors intended. The provinces of Poznan and Pomorze showed a large Polish majority. They did so even before the last war, when they returned Polish members to the German Reichstag. They have been ruthlessly Germanized, and it would certainly be the "freely expressed wish" of their present inhabitants that they remain German. It will, perhaps, be said that the "wish" to be genuinely "free" would have to be expressed in a plebiscite after the war, that the ballot would be held under neutral supervision, and that all those who were expelled by the Germans must be allowed to return and take part in the ballot, just as the Upper Silesians who resided outside their province were allowed to return for the plebiscite which was held in 1921. But many, very many, of the Poles who lived in Poznan and Pomorze two years ago cannot return, because they have fallen in battle or have been shot or hanged by the Germans or have perished in German concentration camps or in Russian places of exile. Besides, plebiscites are often dangerous. They are usually accompanied by terrorism and may lead to armed clashes —as the Upper Silesian plebiscite did. They provide cover for the creation of armed gangs which may develop into armies. The revival of German militarism began on the German eastern frontier—and more especially in Upper Silesia.—*Editorial. Nineteenth Century. S. '41. p. 143.*

In respect to [the question whether the constituent states of a successful federation must be democracies with a common bill of rights], we know of no federal union which counts both democracies and dictatorships among its member states. To understand why such a combination would be unworkable, one needs but imagine the situation we would have here in the United States if the Constitution did not guarantee to all citizens of the Union the basic rights of man—freedom of speech, press, religion and peaceful association—and if New York State were governed by a man with Hitler's powers and purposes, Ohio by a Stalin and Illinois by a Mussolini, while the states in between sought to remain democracies.

In such conditions, no books or periodicals or papers could possibly enjoy free circulation throughout the whole Union, there could be no such thing as Union-wide public opinion or Union-wide parties, the dictatorial states would cast their votes as a solid bloc; the democratic states would be at a very dangerous disadvantage, as exposed to aggression from their autocratic neighbors as the democracies in Europe. The United States could not possibly continue on such a basis. Even the League of Nations couldn't. As *Union Now* says: "We organize a tug of war, not a government, when we arrange for those who believe that government is made for the people to pull together with those who believe the opposite."

After all, our purpose in making this Union is the same for which the people of the Thirteen States established the Constitution—"to secure the blessings of liberty for ourselves and our posterity," not to make the world safe for autocracy. We of the democratic world do not seek to impose our common bill of rights on others by force, but we do mean to defend those rights and keep others from depriving us of them by force. The British and American democracies are now seeking to defend these common rights separately. We proposed to put behind that defense the strength that only Union brings.—*Clarence K. Streit, Author of "Federal Union Now," and Patrick Welch. Decision. Mr. '41. p. 23-4.*

Unless the United States decides . . . to restrict its activities to its own continental boundaries, accepting a shrunken economy and reduced standards of living, it will have to undertake either the task of Western Hemisphere "integration," with all the dangers implied in a policy of nationalistic expansion, or else accept its share of responsibility for reconstruction of the world on universal lines, cutting across regional and continental units. To many Americans this task of reconstruction may appear a staggering, in fact an impossible task. It is, without doubt, a staggering task. But in weighing its possibilities, we must always remember that Hitler is not only ready but eager to undertake the reorganization of Europe and the world on the Nazi pattern. Failure to meet the Nazi challenge in these universal terms may mean the defeat of the Western powers—not on the field of battle, but by default—because the Western people will then have demonstrated that they lack the courage, the vision and the fortitude to set forth, as earlier explorers, pilgrims, and pioneers in their history have done, toward democracy's new horizons. There may be no new lands to discover, no new resources to tap. But we have only begun to explore the possibilities of human cooperation—not for war destruction but for peace construction—to promote social welfare. Out of this travail, if we all can pass the supreme test imposed on us by today's events, life may come, instead of death. As Carl Sandburg said of the Civil War: "Death was in the air. So was birth. What was dying, men did not know. What was being born, none could say."—*Vera Micheles Dean, Research Director, Foreign Policy Association. Survey Graphic. Je. '41. p. 346.*

This set of basic principles, appropriately called "The Atlantic Charter," deals with commercial policy in its fourth point which reads, "They will endeavor, with due respect for their existing obligations, to further the enjoyment by all states, great or small, victor or vanquished, of access, on equal terms, to the trade and to the raw materials of the world which are needed for their economic prosperity."

This categorical statement of the essentials of post-war commercial policy requires no interpretation. I should, however, like to emphasize its meaning and significance.

The basic conception is that your government is determined to move towards the creation of conditions under which restrictive and unconscionable tariffs, preferences, and discriminations are things of the past; under which no nation should seek to benefit itself at the expense of another; and under which destructive trade warfare shall be replaced by cooperation for the welfare of all nations.

The Atlantic Declaration means that every nation has a right to expect that its legitimate trade will not be diverted and throttled by towering tariffs, preferences, discriminations, or narrow bilateral practices. Most fortunately we have already done much to put our own commercial policy in order. So long as we adhere and persistently implement the principles and policies which made possible the enactment of the Trade Agreements Act, the United States will not furnish, as it did after the last war, an excuse for trade-destroying and trade-diverting practices.

The purpose so simply set forth in the Atlantic Declaration is to promote the economic prosperity of all nations "great or small, victor or vanquished." Given this purpose and the determination to act in accordance with it, the means of attaining this objective will always be found. It is a purpose which does not have its origin primarily in altruistic conceptions. It is inspired by the realization, so painfully forced on us by the experiences of the past and of the present, that in the long run no nation can prosper by itself or at the expense of others and that no nation can live unto itself alone.—*Sumner Welles, Under Secretary of State. Address, October* 7, 1941. *Govt. Ptg. Office. Washington, D.C. p.* 10.

In any discussion of post-war plans, it is increasingly important to bear in mind that what is spoken of as peace aims is not this or that program of concrete territorial, economic or financial measures, but a general concept of the kind of international society that might be developed upon cessation of hostilities. Without such a general concept of the objectives to be sought at a peace conference, no catalogue of peace aims, however comprehensive or elaborate, would possess the universal appeal that alone could insure its practical realization and continued effectiveness. Even if the second World War be viewed solely as a struggle for strategic bases, markets, and raw materials—as it is by many—it must be recognized that this conflict will determine the political, social, and economic shape of the world in accordance with the general philosophy of life formulated or practiced by the victor.

In a very profound sense, also, peace aims are a part of military strategy. For if at a given moment the tide of battle should turn against Germany, the German people—many of whom agree with Hitler's thesis that the Reich was inveigled

into surrender in 1918 by President Wilson's Fourteen Points—
may be expected to fight on to the bitter end, since they fear that
defeat might mean the partition of Germany or its reduction to
a status of economic inferiority.   The Western powers must no
longer indulge in high-flown platitudes about international cooperation and justice for all, but should demonstrate, in the
midst of war, what they intend to do once the war is over.   As
Ernest Bevin has said, it is "no good going to the teeming millions of Europe . . . talking merely Gladstonian liberty.   We
have to offer a new feeling of hope, and example is better than
precept."—*Vera Micheles Dean, Research Director, Foreign
Policy Association.   Survey Graphic.   Je. '41. p.* 341.

When we have defeated Hitler, and destroyed this Nazi bid
for world dominion, we must set up conditions which will prevent the rise of new Hitlers.   We have seen how frightfully
near to destruction our civilization can be brought by total war.
We can not permit total war; that way leads to the road of
darkness and night, and we, here in America, must lead the
way to peace, to a restoration of a reign of law.

But again let me emphasize that war, unless guaranteed by
force, is helpless.   Some time, somewhere, an international order
may emerge which need not rely on force, but that time, unhappily, is a long way off.

In the interim, a justly conducted, peace-loving force must
intervene to save the world from self-destruction.   The foundation of such a force, as I have indicated, must be the control
of the seas by the United States and Great Britain.

Other nations of similar peaceful inclinations, and lacking
in aggressive designs, could be joined to them, and thus the
beginning would be made leading toward the restoration of
international law; the policing of the highways, the opening of
the door of opportunity to all peoples and the achievement of a
world in which war, at last, shall be abandoned as an instrument
of national policy.

I make no claims for this proposal as a counsel of perfection. It is an attempt, obviously, to deal with the world as we find it; with facts as they are. But of this thing we can be sure, that respect for law must be restored if the world is to recover and popular government is to be preserved. And the only kind of peace which is available in this world in which we live is the kind of peace that can and will be enforced through the superior power of those nations that love justice and seek after peace.—*Franklin Knox, Secretary of the Navy. Address before the American Bar Association, October* 1, 1941. *New York Times. O.* 2, '41. *p.* 4.

Canada's place in a world divided into regional groups would naturally be in the Union of American States. Traditionally and historically, however, we have been associated with another group which cuts across geographical lines, the British Commonwealth of Nations. As these two great international organizations are presently organized, there would be no incompatibility, either legal or political, in Canada belonging to them both. But the situation might be different if both or either of them were organized on a federal basis. As presently constituted, neither the Union of American States nor the British Commonwealth of Nations has any legal right to control the action of its members, let alone citizens of the latter. The British Commonwealth of Nations is an association of free nations whose only links are now a common crown and a tradition of close political and economic cooperation. The Union of American States is also an association of free nations. The latter are united by a complex pattern of treaty arrangements; but it is a characteristic of the system that member states are under no obligation to accept these treaties. Argentina, for example, has only ratified five out of 72 Pan American conventions. It is a fact, moreover, that none of these treaties contain important political commitments; and none of them are incompatible with membership in the British Commonwealth of Nations. If, however, either system were organized on a federal basis, member states as well as the citizens of the latter would be bound to the international federal authority; and the heretofore sovereign states would no longer be free to follow independent lines of action. These obligations might be such as to render membership in both systems incompatible. But the conclusion does not necessarily follow; for the federal idea is capable of almost indefinite extensions; and there is no reason why Canada could not be a member of one system in respect to certain things and a member of the other in respect to others. The problem, after all, is only one of dividing powers between various authorities.—*John P. Humphrey, Faculty of Law, McGill University. Canadian Forum. O. '41. p. 201-2.*

I have, as the House knows, hitherto consistently deprecated the formulation of peace aims or war aims, however you put it, by His Majesty's Government at this stage and I deprecate it at this time when the end of the war is not in sight and when the conflict sways to and fro with alternating fortunes and while conditions and associations at the end of the war are unforeseeable. But joint declaration by Great Britain and the United States of America is an event of a totally different nature.

Although principles in declaration have long been familiar to the British and American democracies, the fact that it is a united declaration sets up a milestone or monument which needs only the stroke of victory to become a permanent part of the history of human progress.

First, the joint declaration does not try to explain how the principles proclaimed by it are to be applied to each and every case which will have to be dealt with when the war comes to an end. It would not be wise for us at this moment to be drawn into laborious discussion as to how it is to fit all the manifold problems with which we shall be faced after the war.

Secondly, the joint declaration does not qualify in any way the various statements of policy which have been made from time to time about development of constitutional government in India, Burma, or any other parts of the British Empire.

We are pledged by the declaration of August, 1940, to help India obtain free and equal partnership in the British Commonwealth with ourselves, subject of course to fulfillment of obligations arising from our long connection with India and our responsibilities to its creeds, races and interests.

Burma is also covered by our considered policy of establishing Burmese self-government and by measures already in progress.

We had in mind primarily restoration of the sovereignty, self-government and national life of the states and nations of Europe now under the Nazi yoke, and the principles which would govern any alterations in the territorial boundaries of countries which may have to be made.—*Prime Minister Winston Churchill. Speech in House of Commons, September 9, 1941. New York Times. S.* 10, '41. *p.* 14.

The fourth point provides for non-discriminatory trade and access by all nations to raw materials. The fifth point sets forth a condition which would alone make such a pledge practical, the condition being high living standards in all countries. It is suggested that international collaboration must supplement national programs in bringing this about. The phraseology of these two points is a little obscure, but the intent is plain enough. The goals set forth were expressed in another joint statement by the President and a British Prime Minister, Mr. MacDonald in 1933, just before the London Economic Conference. They were not translated into practical policy at that Conference, and this failure, it is now recognized, was a contributory cause of the war. The difficulties of 1933 were due to the aftermath of the great depression of 1929. There will be equal if not greater difficulties to surmount after the war is **over.**

The Atlantic Declaration looks to a world in which the whole of the present system of quotas, allotments, exchange controls and bilateral trade agreements will have to be scrapped. High protective tariffs will have to go, otherwise nations seeking raw materials in the high tariff countries will not be able to obtain the exchange with which to buy them. It is this consequence which makes it essential for high tariff countries like the United States to encourage countries with lower living standards and lower costs of production to raise those standards and increase those costs if internal economic dislocations are not to be created.

The Atlantic Declaration, also, looks to a world in which foreign exchanges are stable, making possible long-term commercial contracts and financial undertakings. The only monetary system which the world has found in the past capable of meeting these conditions is the gold standard. Since the United States holds practically the entire world's supply of gold, the success or failure of this post-war endeavor rests squarely upon the United States.

The Atlantic Declaration looks finally to a world in which nations do not attempt to maintain prices artificially above world levels. This is the other side to the principle that nations with low standards of living must have those standards raised. Much of the American domestic program must be scrapped if this condition is to be fulfilled in the post-war world. For example the entire farm program of parity prices, that is to say prices which do not depend upon existing conditions but upon prices current in the days before the first German War, will have to be abandoned.

There was no American economic adviser present at the Atlantic meeting so one cannot be certain that all the consequences of the two economic points were explored. One wonders whether either President Roosevelt or Mr. Churchill saw that they were passing sentence of exile on economic conceptions held by nearly all left-wing groups and were advocating a return to the principles proclaimed dead and buried for the past ten years, the principles of competitive liberal capitalism.—*Denys Smith, National Review (London). O. '41. p. 449-50.*

We are left to guess what manner of "wider scheme" the signatories of the Declaration have in mind. There would seem to be two main possibilities—a new League of Nations with, perhaps, a revised Covenant, or some form of Federal Union. A League of Nations so constituted as to perpetuate an Allied victory might serve a useful purpose, though it would be more honest to call it by its proper name—that is to say, the anti-German alliance. But a League which would eliminate the difference between victor and vanquished would thereby undo the victory and help to bring on the Third World War. A League that would promote international disarmament would be promoting German rearmament. Armaments are relative, not absolute. It makes no difference, ultimately, whether Germany rearms until her armament equals that of the other Powers, or whether the other Powers disarm until their armament equals that of the Germans. Universal disarmament would make the Germans master of Europe, for, with her central position, her resources, her discipline, her size, and the military prowess of her people, she will always have the initial advantage in every conflict, unless there exists in Europe a Power, or a coalition of Powers, maintaining a permanent armed preponderance and holding strategic positions that will make immediate and decisive action possible the moment the German danger shows itself again.

The schemes that go under the generic term "Federal Union" would, if carried out, also make Germany master of Europe. "Federal Union" is, in fact, one of Germany's principal war aims. If she wins the war, she will unite the nations of Europe in one federation, under her own leadership. If the nations of Europe united of their own accord, Germany will, in a short time, dominate them unless they are united against her. But in that case the "union" will be but an anti-German alliance. It will be said that if Germany is disarmed, she will have been rendered unable to make herself master in a federally united Europe. But if she herself is one of the federal states, she would have equality of status with the other states in the federal government, in the federal court—and in the federal armed forces. Without this equality the union would not be a union at all, or at least it would exclude Germany, and would, therefore, be an alliance. There is a case for regional federation— between Poland and Czechoslovakia, and perhaps Rumania, or between the Balkan States. The former federation would be directed against Germany. The German danger would be its *raison d'être*. It would be one of those "precautions" Mr. Eden referred to in his address. The purpose of a Balkan Federation would be to preserve the Balkans from interference on the part of the Great Powers, especially Germany and Italy. If Germany joined either federation she would automatically become master thereof. Indeed, any federation *with* Germany would lead to annexation *by* Germany. Federal Union would give Germany in peace what she will have failed to gain by war. Federal Union, which has influential exponents on both sides of the Atlantic, is not a piece of harmless crankery. It is a positive menace, for if Great Britain and the Allies win the war, they will lose the peace if the principles of Federal Union are accepted. Federal Union, like a revived League of Nations and like international disarmament, can only have one consequence—the Third World War.—*Editorial. F. A. Voigt. Nineteenth Century. S. '41. p.* 148-9.

1. We must have Europe and its colonies. . . Germany will spread its might far beyond its borders in the East as well as in the South-East. . . . We have a right to South America. . . . Natural instincts bid all living beings not merely conquer their enemies but destroy them. ("Hitler Speaks")

2. This struggle will open to us the door to permanent mastery of the world. . . . There will still be the class of subject

alien races. We need not hesitate to call them the modern slave class. ("Hitler Speaks")

3. The day of small states is past. . . . We do not seek equality but mastery. We shall not waste time over minority rights and other such ideological abortions of sterile democracy. ("Hitler Speaks")

4. After the end of the war Germany must digest the incorporated territories. From the economic point of view this means adjustment to the German economy. ("Voelkischer Beobachter," August 20, 1940)

Our superior industrial products will be sold at very low prices to the whole world and will for example cause the United States to have not 7,000,000 but 30-40,000,000 unemployed. Mr. Roosevelt will then beg the Fuehrer on his knees to purchase from the United States not manufactured products but raw materials at prices which we will dictate. (Nazi Agriculture Minister Darrè to party officials, May 1940).

5. All soil and industrial property of inhabitants of non-German origin will be confiscated without exception and distributed among the worthy members of the Party and soldiers who were accorded honors for bravery in this war. . . . This German aristocracy will have slaves assigned to it, these slaves to be their property and to consist of landless, non-German nationals. We actually have in mind a modern form of mediaeval slavery which we must and will introduce. . . . Work must be as cheap as possible in order that our economic conquest may spread extensively and rapidly. (Darrè).

6. The world can only be ruled by fear. . . . Terror is the most effective political instrument. . . . I recognize no moral law in politics. . . . There will be no license, no free space, in which the individual belongs to himself. ("Hitler Speaks")

7. The German navy will be expanded to a strength worthy of a world power. It will carry the German flag and the German name over the face of the globe. (Admiral Raeder, January 28, 1941

8. War is eternal. War is universal. War is life. ("Hitler Speaks")

After the war, armament will go on at the present rate bringing new world power to Germany. ("Deutsche Allgemeine Zeitung," September 2, 1940)—*From article "The Eight-Point Plan and Hitler's New Order," comparing the Churchill-Roosevelt Atlantic Declaration with eight similar points given in Hitler's words as quoted from Hermann Rauschning's "Hitler Speaks," and from other authentic sources. Conscience (India). S. 18, '41. p. 337-8.*

That a federation of the democracies, that is, of like-minded people, may be the best way to begin a workable world organization of nations is, it seems to me, indisputable. But when the plan is limited first to countries of one predominant race, Britain to exclude India and her other colored subjects from the union, and further when the plan is limited to one language, what we have in essence is a union of white English-speaking people against the rest of the world and from this conclusion there is no escape. This is how the plan will inevitably appear to China, to Japan, and to all other oriental peoples.

What will be the consequences of this? It takes no prophet to tell. Japan and China will unite, partly by force of Japan's pressure, partly because China sees herself excluded from federation elsewhere, and China will become Japan's power house. There will then be in effect a colored union against a white union. India will certainly join the former since she is purposely excluded from the latter.

We seem in every devastating war to sow the seeds for the next war. Here then are the seeds for the greatest war the human race has yet seen, the war of the white races against the colored. In a subtle form this war has been going on for centuries. But in this plan for the federation of white English-speaking peoples, excluding all others, we have the scheme made clear for the really great world war.

It is a measureless misfortune that Mr. Streit does not know China except in a superficial way. The Chinese people are a thoroughly democratic people, accustomed to self-government and fitted by centuries of essential democracy for participation in just such a federation. Mr. Streit does not know this. He has the ordinary prejudices of the white man and he has formed his plan upon his prejudices. But these prejudices are dangerous wherever they are found. A federation based upon the deepest prejudices of the human race today can end only in further disaster. Our leaders ought to guide us away from these blind prejudices and not further into them.

The advocates of Mr. Streit's plan will protest that prejudice has nothing to do with it, that the real reason for the exclusion of China from the federation of the democracies is an economic one, that China's economy is so different from ours it makes a real federation impossible. This is simply not true. China is very ready to make changes in her currency, and is alive to all possible improvement in herself. No one who has seen the China of the past twenty-five years can doubt her ability to change and adapt. Were China invited to make a third major member of this federation, the federation would gain from her presence and once and for all Japan would be robbed of the opportunity to use China for the development of her own power. Moreover, China's resources would be allied to those of the United States and English-speaking Britain.

Most important of all, the union would cut across the prejudice of race and would prove that the leaders of the world are able to unite on rational bases. One doubts the arguments of economics these days. Ideas, beliefs, feelings seem far more powerful. And nothing will convince the average Chinese that it is for purely economic reasons alone that his country is excluded by the two most powerful white countries in the world today when they unite. He will not believe it and he will be right. On the day that the United States and the white English-speaking part of Britain unite without China, democracy will be dead in the western hemisphere.—*Letter by Pearl S. Buck, Author of "The Good Earth." Asia. S. '41. p. 524.*

PREAMBLE:—

We hold these truths to be, if not self-evident, then certainly based on that natural law which is the eternal Law of God as discovered by human reason:

That there exists an equality of rights among all nations, large or small, strong or weak, to life and independence;

That nevertheless the origin of the human family requires that there be acknowledged an *organic unity* within which this equality of rights finds its expression and achieves its end;

That this organic unity of nations demands that the peoples be governed by a rule of law and not by the rule of force;

That this organic unity is broken up by the strivings of *nationalism* bent on achieving its particular aims to the detriment of the common good;

That this organic unity is also disturbed by the doctrine of absolute and unlimited sovereignty;

That "one nation's will to live must never be tantamount to a death sentence for another" (Pius XII);

That a spirit of international responsibility, of a hunger and thirst after justice, and a universal love must be the guiding forces of relations between nations;

That, these things being so, all the peoples of the world enjoy the following rights:

BILL OF RIGHTS:

I.   The right of economic and political security in the lives, homes, and means of decent livelihood of every person in the world.

II.   The right to be delivered from the *slavery of armaments* which exist either to rob others of their rights or for defense against such robbery.

III.   The right to demand an equitable, wise, and unanimous *revision of treaties* which impair the equality of all nations.

IV.   The right to remove by common action the consequences of past *imperialist aggressions*.

V.   The right of free access to raw materials and of *free economic intercourse* among all the peoples of the world without exception.

VI.   The right of denying to powerful aggregations of capital within the nations of an unlimited self-regulation of *international economic activities* not subject to any law.

VII.   The right of the equal protection of law everywhere in the world for equitable *treatment of laborers*, especially decent conditions of labor, a living wage, reasonable hours, and the abolition of peonage, of child labor, and other economic inequalities.

VIII.   The right of *small nations* that the demands, even legitimate, of larger nations yield before the claims of an organic order which respects the equality of all nations.

IX.   The right of all peoples to require, as a matter of international concern, that all associated states respect the following individual rights:

The right of freedom of conscience and of worship before the State;

The right of freedom of expression within the law;

The right of free association, of free assembly, and of free petition of grievances;

The right of private property; and of being secure against unlawful seizures and confiscations;

The right of freedom of education according to the wishes of the parent;

The right to be tried according to the law and to be secure against cruel and unusual punishments;

The right of ethnic and religious minorities to enjoy equal
     opportunities for the development of their common
     humanity.—*Rev. Wilfred Parsons, S.J. Catholic Uni-*
versity of America. "America's Peace Aims." Catholic Associ-
ation for International Peace. '41. p. 23-4.

For forty years there has been convincing and steadily growing evidence of the fact that the people of the United States
were ready and willing to assume a commanding part in the
organization of the civilized world in order to protect prosperity
and international peace. Ever since the twentieth century began,
each President of the United States, no matter to which of the
major political parties he belonged, placed himself on record
as strongly in support of international agreement among civilized
nations for the security of a rapidly advancing international
economy and social order. Not only have these fundamental
principles been supported by Presidents William McKinley,
Theodore Roosevelt, William Howard Taft, Woodrow Wilson,
Warren Gamaliel Harding, Calvin Coolidge, Herbert Hoover
and Franklin Delano Roosevelt, but they have been endorsed
specifically and emphatically in the declarations of principle
adopted by each of the major political parties at one national
party convention after another. Moreover the Congress of the
United States in June, 1910, by an impressively unanimous vote
supported and defined this policy of international leadership.
In 1915 the Legislature of the State of Massachusetts and in
1941 the Legislature of the State of North Carolina took like
action.

Why is it, then, that nothing has been done? How is it
possible under these circumstances for a small minority of office-
holders at Washington to defeat the aims and ambitions of the
American people in their search for prosperity and peace? Why
has this small minority at Washington gone unpunished? It has
been able to prevent execution of the expressed will of the
American people. It has defeated the plan for the judicial set-

tlement of international disputes which had its origin in American statesmanship. President McKinley's far-sighted statement in his truly great speech of September 5, 1901, was denied and affronted by three successive tariff acts—the Payne-Aldrich Act of 1909, the Fordney-McCumber Act of 1922, and the Hawley-Smoot Act of 1930, the last named of which reached the very apex of folly. These three tariff acts certainly contributed powerfully through their narrow and almost bigoted nationalism to the American trade depression and to the economic and financial collapse which began in 1929. Unfortunately, as far back as 1903 Joseph Chamberlain had led the way toward similar action by the government of Great Britain.

No statement more contrary to recorded fact could be made than that international isolation is the traditional policy of the American government and the American people. The truth is the exact opposite. With the exception of the government and people of Great Britain, no modern government and no modern people have had so constant, so numerous and so powerful international relations, economic, social and intellectual, in every part of the world as have the government and people of the United States. The shades of Benjamin Franklin and of Thomas Jefferson, of John Adams and of Alexander Hamilton, of Henry Clay and of Ralph Waldo Emerson, of Samuel B. F. Morse and of Cyrus W. Field, of Alexander Graham Bell and of Thomas A. Edison, would be astounded to learn that the way to mind their own business was to keep aloof and apart from every other people and every other nation. Let him who still doubts read the impressive record of the recent relations of the United States to world organization in *International Conciliation* for September, 1939, and for June, 1940.—*Nicholas Murray Butler, President, Columbia University. International Conciliation. Je. '41. p. 567-8.*

The ceaseless changes wrought in human society by science, industry and economics, as well as by the spiritual, social and intellectual forces which impregnate all cultures, make political and geographical isolation of nations hereafter impossible. The organic life of the human race is at last indissolubly unified and can never be severed, but it must be politically ordained and made subject to law. Only a government capable of discharging all the functions of sovereignty in the executive, legislative and judicial spheres can accomplish such a task. Civilization now requires laws, in the place of treaties, as instruments to regulate commerce between peoples. The intricate conditions of modern life have rendered treaties ineffectual and obsolete, and made laws essential and inevitable. The age of treaties is dead; the age of laws is here.

Governments, limited in their jurisdiction to local geographical areas, can no longer satisfy the needs or fulfil the obligations of the human race. Just as feudalism served its purpose in human history and was superseded by nationalism, so has nationalism reached its apogee in this generation and yielded its hegemony in the body politic to internationalism. The first duty of government is to protect life and property, and when governments cease to perform this function, they capitulate on the fundamental principle of their raison d'être. Nationalism, moreover, is no longer able to preserve the political independence or the territorial integrity of nations, as recent history so tragically confirms. Sovereignty is an ideological concept without geographical barriers. It is better for the world to be ruled by an international sovereignty of reason, social justice and peace than by diverse national sovereignties organically incapable of preventing their own dissolution by conquest. Mankind must pool its resources of defense if civilization is to endure.

History has revealed but one principle by which free peoples, inhabiting extensive territories, can unite under one government without impairing their local autonomy. That principle is federation, whose virtue preserves the whole without destroying its parts and strengthens its parts without jeopardizing the whole. Federation vitalizes all nations by endowing them with security and freedom to develop their respective cultures without menace of foreign domination. It regards as sacrosanct man's personality, his rights as an individual and as a citizen and his role as a partner with all other men in the common enterprise of building civilization for the benefit of mankind. It suppresses the crime of war by reducing to the ultimate minimum the possibility of its occurrence. It renders unnecessary the further paralyzing expenditure of wealth for belligerent activity, and cancels through the ages the mortgages of war against the fortunes and services of men. It releases the full energies, intelligence and assets of society for creative, ameliorative and redemptive work on behalf of humanity. It recognizes man's morning vision of his destiny as an authentic potentiality. It apprehends the entire human race as one family, human beings everywhere as brothers and all nations as component parts of an indivisible community.

There is no alternative to the federation of all nations except endless war. No substitute for the Federation of the World can organize the international community on the basis of freedom and permanent peace. Even if continental, regional or ideological federations were attempted. the governments of these federations, in an effort to make impregnable their separate defenses, would be obliged to maintain stupendously competitive armies and navies, thereby condemning humanity indefinitely to exhaustive taxation, compulsory military service and ultimate carnage, which history reveals to be not only criminally futile but positively avoidable through judicious foresight in federating all nations. No nation should be excluded from membership in the Federation of the World that is willing to suppress its military, naval and air forces, retaining only a constabulary sufficient to police its territory and to maintain order within its jurisdiction, provided that the eligible voters of that nation are permitted the free expression of their opinions at the polls.—*From "The Declaration of the Federation of the World," a joint resolution adopted by the General Assembly of North Carolina, March 13, 1941. International Conciliation. Je. '41. p.587-9.*

The English people seem ready for some sort of union. They were passionate believers in the League of Nations, led by Eden. The conquered people of Europe are ready. China is ready. Practically the whole world seems ready, except the followers of militarists and perhaps ourselves.

The militarists are seeking world government by the other route—conquest—at our expense. We in this country are still hesitating about any world government at all. Yet history is running true to form; for only by suffering have people ever come to enlarge the peace group. We did not suffer enough in the last World War to be willing to sacrifice a small part of our sovereignty in order to safeguard our freedom. In other words, we refused (or rather a minority of the Senate refused) to follow Wilson in the voluntary route toward world peace. That is why Germany has taken the bit in her teeth and is now trying to get world peace by the conquest route. Hitler has virtually said that "the voluntary way, Wilson's way, didn't work; so now we will try my way—the conquest way." . . .

Clarence Streit has worked out a detailed plan for a world government, probably the best plan so far suggested, and the most appealing for Americans as he takes the American government as his model. It has met with wider popular acceptance than any other and must be reckoned with when the time arrives for choosing among the various plans then available.

Several other plans—at least half a dozen—have been suggested. Among them is that of Professor Ludwig Mises, who has the advantage of first-hand familiarity with European problems. He would add to the Streit plan for uniting democracies, a union of Middle Europe covering a wide strip between Germany and Russia, postponing a world government to a later date. He stresses as one of the causes of discontent, the restrictions which have been imposed on migration. This problem, like the problem of restriction of trade, is one which in any international organization must be faced and solved, like the problem of free trade, and of minorities. The problem of sanctions is perhaps the biggest problem of all. Its solution may involve an international air force with the prohibition of all national air forces.

Whatever may be the wisest plan, we must make use of the valuable experience of the League of Nations and entrust many details to those like Roosevelt and Churchill whose experience has fitted them, perhaps above all others, for the great task.

Perhaps we have got to have another, a third World War, before we can get dinned into the brains of a sufficient number of people what is needed, and that there is no other way. In that case, we shall have to suffer worse bombings. A science writer even now tells of plans for developing a "ten-pound bomb" which would blast a hole twenty-five miles in diameter and a mile deep and would wreck every structure within one hundred miles.

The first effort—the League of Nations—we regard as a failure. If so, our first effort in this country to do what George Washington wanted, was also a failure—the Articles of Confederation. After that "failure" we went through what John Fiske called "the critical period" of our history when we didn't know whether we could maintain the Union that had been started in such a faint-hearted manner. But thanks to the wisdom of Washington, Hamilton, and Benjamin Franklin, and the other great men in those days, we founded our country on a stronger organization principle, the Constitution of the United States. So internationally, we are now going through a "critical period."—*Irving Fisher, Professor Emeritus, Yale University. Federal Union World. N. '41. p.3-4.*

There is, I suggest, a real danger that we may again be led astray unless we soberly confront the issues as history is shaping them for us. We have to avoid the temptations (1) to believe that there can be any attempt to return to the pre-war world, and (2) to accept those siren voices which would lead us into enthusiasm for some vast but simple formula, whether it be a

federal union, an Anglo-American union or the world state. We
have got to make up our minds that the building of a peace
which will endure is going to be a hard and complicated matter,
unlikely to be accomplished at a single stroke, more likely to be
attained by a long series of experiments in which there will be
failures as well as successes.

If we are to approach our problem realistically, there are, I
believe, certain principles which, in Justice Holmes's phrase,
we must accept as the "inarticulate major premises" of our thinking. I state them barely, though each, for proper appreciation,
requires a full analysis. They are:

1. The epoch when liberalism could be identified with laissez-
faire is over. As a consequence we have entered into the epoch
of planned economy. The pivotal authority in planning is bound
to be the state.

2. No state can remain democratic unless it plans for the
many and not for the few. To do so it needs to own and probably itself to operate the essential instruments of production.
Where these remain in private hands they assume the character
of *imperia in imperio* incompatible with the people's sovereignty.

3. No state can now hope to live a self-sufficient life. Interdependence means the organization of collective security, and
collective security means the recognition of the need for common decision on matters of common concern. But because interdependence is new, it is at present the part of wisdom to approach
it empirically, seeking in an evolutionary way to build upon our
wartime experience rather than to attempt any large-scale experiments for which men are not yet wholly prepared.

It is, however, already clear that the duty of economic sanctions against an aggressor must be universally accepted and that
military sanctions, which shall include the leasing of appropriate
naval and air bases on the Anglo-American model must be re-
gionally organized.

4. The lease-lend principle is not less applicable in peace
than in war. It implies an obligation on the part of the richer

states to assist the poorer states in the development of a higher standard of life.

5. In the making of peace, the democracies are entitled to safeguard in the defeated states the conditions which are necessary for the fulfillment of the Four Freedoms. In particular they are bound to destroy the social and economic foundations of German and Japanese militarism.

6. In the making of peace Great Britain and the United States must recognize the inevitability of revolutionary uprisings in the defeated and occupied countries. Subject to their acceptance of the Four Freedoms, Great Britain and America are not enabled to prescribe to these countries either the form or substance of their political and economic organization.

7. It is urgent for us all to understand that this war marks a turning point in history as decisive in its reshaping of our habits and traditions as the Reformation or the French Revolution. Either we adapt ourselves to this recognition, with a consequential power to make the necessary changes by consent, or we refuse to make the adaptation, in which case, even our victory will be no more than the prelude to a long epoch of chaos and confusion, in which much of its possible fruits will be thrown away.

The United States, if I may say so, has a quite special contribution to make in this regard. Born as a refuge from oppression, united by a war for freedom, accustomed from its outset to affirm the rights of man, it has the experience, not less than the obligation, to lead mankind into the new epoch. The process will be long, for men are not easily habituated to a freedom they have rarely experienced.

But if Americans are prepared to be as patient as they have been generous, they have it in their power to make men see what it is that has made Washington and Jefferson, Woodrow Wilson and Franklin Roosevelt a part of the central flame which burns at the heart of the world.—*Harold J. Laski, Professor of Political Science, University of London. New York Times. Ja.* 18, '42. *p.6E.*

BIBLIOGRAPHY

An asterisk (*) preceding a reference indicates that the article or a part of it has been reprinted in this book. (F) or (A) following a reference indicates material for or against the aspect under which it is classified.

BIBLIOGRAPHIES

Johnsen, Julia E. comp. Bibliography. *In* her International federation of democracies (proposed). p. 239-63. (Reference Shelf. Vol. 14, no. 8) H. W. Wilson Co. N.Y. Ap. '41.

Phelps, Edith M. ed. Union of the United States and the British Commonwealth of Nations. *In* her University debaters' annual, 1940-1941. p. 271-80. H. W. Wilson Co. N.Y. '41.

GENERAL REFERENCES

BOOKS AND PAMPHLETS

Adamic, Louis. Two-way passage. 328p. Harper & Bros. N.Y. '41.

Angell, Norman. America's dilemma: alone or allied? 226p. Harper & Bros. N.Y. '41.

Catholic Association for International Peace. World society; a joint report. Charles O'Donnell, ed. 48p. The Association. 1312 Massachusetts Av. N.W. Wash. D.C. '41.

Cecil of Chelwood, Edgar A. R. Gascoyne-Cecil, 1st Viscount. Great experiment; an autobiography. 390p. Jonathan Cape. Lond. '41.

Commission To Study the Bases of a Just and Durable Peace of the Federal Council of the Churches of Christ in America. Just and durable peace; data material and discussion questions. 64p. The Commission. 297 4th Av. N.Y. '41.

Corbett, P. E. Post-war worlds. 211p. (I.P.R. Inquiry Series) Farrar & Rinehart. N.Y. '42.

Cromwell, James H. R. Pax Americana; American democracy and world peace. 94p. A. Kroch & Son. Chic. '41.

Dean, Vera Micheles. Struggle for world order. 96p. (Headline Books no. 32) Foreign Policy Association. 22 E. 38th St. N.Y. N. '41.

Howe, Quincy. World revolution comes to America. 13p. mim. Institute of Public Affairs. Univ. of Virginia. Charlottesville. Je. 24, '41.

Ingersoll, Ralph. America is worth fighting for. 152p. Bobbs-Merrill Co. Indianapolis. '41.

Institute for Advanced Study, Princeton University. World organization, 1920-1940. 39p. The Institute. Princeton, N.J. Prepared in cooperation with the Rockefeller Institute at Princeton. '41.

Institute of World Affairs. Proceedings. 18:299p. '40. War and society. The Institute. Univ. of Southern California. Los Angeles. '41.

Kallen, H. M. Future of peace. 39p. (Public Policy Pamphlet no. 34) Univ. of Chicago Press. Chic. D. '41.

Laves, Walter H. C. ed. Foundations of a more stable world order. 192p. Univ. of Chicago Press. Chic. '41.

*Lerner, Max. If we own the future. *In* his Ideas for the ice age. p. 58-79. Viking Press. N.Y. '41.
Same. Antioch Review. 1:270-90. S. '41.

Lindal, W. J. Two ways of life; freedom or tyranny. 154p. Ryerson Press. Toronto. '40.

Manden, Linden A. Foundations of modern world society. 910p. Stanford Univ. Press. Stanford University, Calif. '41.

Muste, A. J. Where are we going? 23p. Fellowship of Reconciliation. 2929 Broadway. N.Y. n.d.

Schuman, Frederick L. Design for power; the struggle for the world. 324p. Alfred A. Knopf. N.Y. '42.

Periodicals

American Mercury. 53:49-55. Jl. '41. Case studies in isolationism; ancient nations followed the path of appeasement, to extinction. Frederick H. Cramer.

Annals of the American Academy. 216:163-77. Jl. '41. New world order. M. J. Bonn.

Annals of the American Academy. 218:141-52. N. '41. Regional aspects of world recovery. Charles C. Colby.

Antioch Review. 1:328-42. S. '41. Lines of action in economic reconstruction. Mordecai Ezekiel.

Antioch Review. 1:343-55. S. '41. Shape of a constitutional economic order. Lewis Corey.

Antioch Review. 1:511-22. D. '41. Notes on the war and the peace. Louis Dolivet.

Asia. 41:437-41. Ag. '41. Postwar imperialism: a democratic solution. Albert Viton.

Contemporary Review. 159:601-9. Je. '41. Faith of democracy. J. A. Spender.

Fortnightly. 156 (n.s. 150):555-9. D. '41. Culture and diplomacy. Roger Lloyd.

*Free World. 1:14-16. O. '41. Dilemmas for a post-war world. Quincy Wright.

Free World. 1:43-9. O. '41. First things first. Norman Angell.

Harvard Guardian. 6:24-8. O. '41. America's war aims. Howard D. Sharpe.

Hibbert Journal. 40:22-33. O. '41. Oneness of the world. Maxwell Garnett.

Institute of International Education News Bulletin. 17:3-5. O. '41. World-mindedness. Stephen P. Duggan.
Same. Association of American Colleges Bulletin. 27:602-4. D. '41.

Institute of International Education News Bulletin. 17:3-5. D. '41. Policing the world. Stephen P. Duggan.

Institute of International Education News Bulletin. 17:3-6. Ja. '42. World economic organization. Stephen P. Duggan.

International Conciliation. 369:193-531. Ap. '41. Commission To Study the Organization of Peace; preliminary report and monographs.

International Conciliation. 371:567-90. Je. '41. Leadership of the United States in world organization for prosperity and peace; statements by leaders of American public opinion, 1901-1941. ed. by Nicholas Murray Butler.
*Joint resolution [North Carolina] providing for a declaration of the federation of the world. p. 586-90.

International Conciliation. 374:683-91. N. '41. Challenge of international lawlessness. Robert H. Jackson.

National Education Association. Journal. 30:257. D. '41. World dream. Joy Elmer Morgan.

Nature. 148:233-5. Ag. 30, '41. International collaboration.

Nature. 148:263-6. S. 6, '41. Anglo-American technical co-operation.

New York Times. p. 2. My. 28, '41. Text of the President's address depicting emergency confronting the nation.

New York Times. p. 4. O. 2, '41. Secretary Knox's address before the Bar Association.

Rotarian. 59:8-9. O. '41. Cave man is still within us; a few reflections on the state of the world. Hendrik van Loon.

Saturday Evening Post. 214:26. Jl. 19, '41. That world feeling.

Spectator (London). 166:392-3. Ap. 11, '41. Security club. Balbus, pseud.
    Discussion. Spectator. 166:448. Ap. 25, '41.

Spectator (London). 167:79-80. Jl. 25, '41. Peace by economics. Mark Sterling.
    Reply. Spectator. 167:156. Ag. 15, '41. L. Zeitlin.

Virginia Quarterly Review. 17, no. 3:321-36. [Jl.] '41. After imperialism, what? Albert Viton.

World Affairs Interpreter. 12:235-46. O. '41. Coming revival of the League of Nations. J. Eugene Harley.

WAR AIMS: AXIS

BOOKS AND PAMPHLETS

Aims of the Nazis. 3p. (Leaflet 4) British Library of Information. 620 5th Av. N.Y. Jl. 16, '41.

Einzig, Paul. Hitler's new order in Europe. 147p. Macmillan. Lond. '41.

Hartley, Livingston. Consequences of an appeasement peace. 11p. American Council on Public Affairs. 2153 Florida Av. Wash. D.C. '41.

Hitler, Adolf. My new order. ed. with commentary by Raoul de Roussy de Sales; with an introduction by Raymond Gram Swing. 1008p. Reynal & Hitchcock. N.Y. '41.

Ludwig, Emil. Germans: double history of a nation. 509p. Little, Brown & Co. Bost. '41.

Rauschning, Hermann. Hitler speaks. 287p. Thomas Nelson & Sons. Toronto. '39.

Rauschning, Hermann. Hitler wants the world! 64p. Argus Press. Lond. '41.

Reveille, Thomas, pseud. Spoil of Europe; the Nazi technique in political and economic conquest. 344p. W. W. Norton & Co. N.Y. '41.
   Digest. Information Service (Federal Council of the Churches of Christ in America). 20:[1-4]. N. 29, '41.

Royal Institute of International Affairs. Europe under Hitler, in prospect and in practice. 45p. Oxford Univ. Press. N.Y. '41.

Strausz-Hupé, Robert. Axis America; Hitler plans our future. 274p. G. P. Putnam's Sons. N.Y. '41.

PERIODICALS

American Magazine. 133:18-19+. Ja. '42. How Hitler plans to enslave Europe. Hugh O'Connor.

Annals of the American Academy. 215:54-60. My. '41. Pan-Asiatic union: a Japanese conception. Shingoro Takaishi.

Asia. 41:422-5. Ag. '41. What Hitler wants in Asia. Fritz Sternberg.

Asia. 41:653-60. N. '41. Hitler means to destroy Japan. Anton Pettenkofer.

Atlantic Monthly. 168:1-8. Jl. '41. American business and Hitler. Douglas Miller.

Atlantic Monthly. 168:12-17. Jl. '41. World or nothing. Herbert Agar.

Business Week. p. 74. Ag. 16, '41. New Nazi plan; division of all the world into three economic parts.

Christian Science Monitor Weekly Magazine Section. p. 2+. Jl. 12, '41. Pattern of Nazi conquest. Joseph C. Harsch.
   Reply with rejoinder. Christian Science Monitor Weekly Magazine Section. p. 15. D. 20, '41. Eleanora B. Carr.

Collier's. 108:20-1+. S. 13, '41. Hitler's peace map. W. B. Courtney.

Congressional Record. 87:A5996. D. 17, '41. Issue; Japan.

Economic Journal (London). 51:1-18. Ap. '41. Hitler's new order in theory and practice. Paul Einzig.

Economist (London). 140:783-5. Je. 14, '41. United States of Europe.

Fortnightly. 156 (n.s. 150):336-47. O. '41. Hitler's pax Germanica; new order plans. Peter F. Drucker.

Fortune. 24:110-12+. N. '41. Geopolitics; Haushofer's sinister pseudo science now rules German foreign policy. Robert Strausz-Hupé.

Fortune. 24:132+. D. '41. Europe: how Germany rules it.

Fortune. 25:48-51+. Ja. '42. Europe: a new economic order rises.

Great Britain and the East. 56:256. Ap. 3, '41. Hegemony of Asia: examination of Japanese claims.

Harper's Magazine. 183:586-97. N. '41. German geopolitics, a workshop for army rule. H. W. Weigert.

Information Service (Federal Council of the Churches of Christ in America). 20:1-4. N. 29, '41. Spoil of Europe, by Thomas Reveille; review.

Nation. 152:333-63. Mr. 22, '41. Survey of two worlds; a Hitler peace, a Hitler defeat; symposium.

Nation. 153:29-32. Jl. 12, '41. Thousand year plan. Peter F. Drucker.
     Same abridged. Reader's Digest. 39:37-40. Ag. '41. Hitler's blueprint for a German Europe.

Nature. 147:755-7. Je. 21, '41. Propaganda in Europe.

Newsweek. 18:25. N. 10, '41. Latin new order; German plans to carve Latin America into five vassal states.

Nineteenth Century. 130:150-5. S. '41. New order in Europe. Edvard Benes.

Pacific Affairs. 14:198-206. Je. '41. Japan's new order in the Pacific. William Magistretti.

Social Research. 8:136-55. My. '41. Control of the conquered. Erich Hula.
     Also separate. 22p. (Studies on War and Peace no. 11). New School for Social Research. 66 W. 12th St. N.Y. '41.

Virginia Quarterly Review. 18, no. 1:135-40. [Ja.] '42. What Nazi methods mean. Dexter Perkins.

ALLIED AIMS AND PRINCIPLES

BOOKS AND PAMPHLETS

American Society of International Law. Proceedings. 1941:9-13. United States and the world situation. Cordell Hull.

Catholic Association for International Peace. America's peace aims; a committee report. 48p. The Association. 1312 Massachusetts Av. N.W. Wash. D.C. '41.

Commission To Study the Organization of Peace. Statement of American proposals for a new world order. 2p. The Commission. 8 W. 40th St. N.Y. Je. 6, '41.

*Commission To Study the Organization of Peace. War and the peace. p. 3-4. mim. (Bul. no. 8) The Commission. 8 W. 40th St. N.Y. Ag. '41.

Davis, Howard Pierce. Obligations of the United States as a world power. 13p. mim. Institute of Public Affairs. Univ. of Virginia. Charlottesville. Je. 24, '41.

England speaks; a symposium. 222p. Macmillan Co. N.Y. '41.

PERIODICALS

Amerasia. 5:425-32. D. '41. Goal beyond victory; lessons of Versailles for the future Pacific settlement. Benjamin H. Kizer.

American Journal of International Law. 35:336-40. Ap. '41. United States and the statement of war aims. Clyde Eagleton.

Annals of the American Academy. 216:117-24. Jl. '41. American leadership in a harsh age. Max Lerner.

Annals of the American Academy. 216:125-34. Jl. '41. Economic union and enduring peace. Otto Tod Mallery.

Atlantic Monthly. 168:575-83. N. '41. Don't do it again. Andrew McFadyean.

Atlantic Monthly. 169:34-41. Ja. '42. Foundations of the peace. Henry A. Wallace.

Catholic World. 153:749. S. '41. America's peace aims: Father Parson's international bill of rights.

Catholic World. 154:54-9. O. '41. Men v. the money-power; problem of after-war reconstruction. T. W. C. Curd.

Christian Century. 58:1494. D. 3, '41. Rabbis issue program of world reconstruction.

Christian Century. 59:75-6. Ja. 21, '42. Preparation for the peace. Oswald Garrison Villard.

Christian Science Monitor Weekly Magazine Section. p. 1-2. Ag. 2, '41. Who owns the future? William Henry Chamberlin.

Christian Science Monitor Weekly Magazine Section. p. 7+. N. 8, '41. When cease firing sounds. Truman L. Kelly.

Commonweal. 34:493-4. S. 12, '41. Views and reviews; reorganization of the world when the war is over. Michael Williams.

Contemporary Review. 160:145-51. S. '41. Vision of the future. Wickham Steed.

Contemporary Review. 160:209-17. O. '41. Issue. Gilbert Murray.

Contemporary Review. 160:273-8. N. '41. Germany and peace. Viscount Cecil.

Contemporary Review. 161:17-21. Ja. '42. Future of the small nations. Emile Cammaerts.

Current History. n.s. 1:397-424. Ja. '42. American war documents; October 30 to December 9, 1941.

Dublin Review. 209:169-82. O. '41, International commerce. Christopher Hollis.

Editorial Research Reports. p. 171-90. Mr. 15, '41. War aims. Buel W. Patch.

Foreign Affairs. 20:282-92. Ja. '42. Restoring trade after the war; suggested remedy for old defects. Herbert Feis.

Foreign Policy Reports. 17:50-68. My. 15, '41. Toward a new world order. Vera Micheles Dean.

Fortnightly. 156 (n.s. 150):209-23, 320-5, 405-13, S.-N. '41. Future of Germany; discussion on the Political and Economic Planning Broadsheet.

Fortnightly. 156 (n.s. 150):1-17. O. '41. Reconstruction and the U.S.S.R. Balbus, pseud.

Fortune. 23:sup. 1-20. Ap. '41. Peace aims; eighth Fortune round table.

Fortune. 23:54-5. My. '41. Future of U.S. foreign policy.

Fortune. 24:45-7+. Ag. '41. This would be victory; a proposed international party. Russell W. Davenport.

Fortune. 24:100+. Ag. '41. Political warfare.

Great Britain and the East. 57:212. O. 2, '41. Rebuilding after the war; message of hope from the allied governments' conference.

Harper's Magazine. 183:206-16. Jl. '41. There'll be some changes made; question of post-war reconstruction. C. Hartley Grattan.

International Conciliation. 373:649-56. O. '41. Freedom of the seas; radio address, September 11, 1941. Franklin D. Roosevelt.
Same. Current History. n.s. 1:218-23. N. '41; *Same* with title Time for active defense is now. Vital Speeches of the Day. 7:738-41. O. 1, '41.

International Conciliation. 376:31-5. Ja. '42. After the war. James T. Shotwell.

Life. 10:84-8+. Ap. 7, '41. Atlantic and America. Walter Lippmann.

Nature. 148:447-9. O. 18, '41. Foundations of a new world order.

New Europe. 1:108-13. Ap. '41. British and allied war and peace aims. Harry N. Howard.

New Republic. 105:297-300. S. 8, '41. Substitute for imperialism.

New Republic. 106:163-84. F. 2, '42. Lessons of last time. George Soule.

New Statesman and Nation. 22:417. N. 15, '41. Chance for political warfare.

New York Times. p. 6E. Ja. 18, '42. Temptations to avoid. Harold J. Laski.

Political Quarterly. 12:237-50. Jl. '41. Prolegomena to peace aims. Barbara Ward.

Political Quarterly. 12:367-79. O. '41. How to make the peace. Leonard Woolf.

Rotarian. 59:8-9. S. '41. Bases for a lasting peace. H. G. Wells.

Rotarian. 60:8-11+. Ja. '42. Americas show the way. Walter B. Pitkin.

Round Table. 31:221-34. Mr. '41. Two orders.

Social Research. 8:267-82. S. '41. War aims and America's aims. Max Ascoli.
Also separate. 18p. (Studies on War and Peace no. 12). New School for Social Research. 66 W. 12th St. N.Y. '41.

Spectator (London). 167:347. O. 10, '41. Post-war League.

Survey Graphic. 30:340-6. Je. '41. Can democracy win the peace? Vera Micheles Dean.

Town Meeting (Bulletin of America's Town Meeting of the Air). 7, no. 5:3-26. N. 17, '41. What kind of peace must we have? John A. Zellers, Norman Thomas, and Dorothy Thompson.

Vital Speeches of the Day. 8:18-21. O. 15, '41. World peace must be enforced. Frank Knox.

Vital Speeches of the Day. 8:34+. N. 1, '41. American merchant ships must be armed; message to Congress, October 9, 1941. Franklin D. Roosevelt.
Same. Current History. n.s. 1:310-13. D. '41.

Vital Speeches of the Day. 8:66-8. N. 15, '41. Shooting has started; Navy Day address, October 27, 1941. Franklin D. Roosevelt.
Same. Current History. n.s. 1:313-16. D. '41.

Vital Speeches of the Day. 8:98-100. D. 1, '41. Address to International Labor Organization, November 6, 1941. Franklin D. Roosevelt.

Vital Speeches of the Day. 8:130. D. 15, '41. War address to joint session of Congress, December 8, 1941. Franklin D. Roosevelt.

Vital Speeches of the Day. 8:131-3. D. 15, '41. Congress and people have accepted the challenge; radio address, December 9, 1941. Franklin D. Roosevelt.

Vital Speeches of the Day. 8:197-9. Ja. 15, '42. Here we are together; address to joint session of Congress, December 26, 1941. Winston Churchill.
Same. International Conciliation. 377:62-9. F. '42; New York Times. p. 4. D. 27, '41.

Yale Review. n.s. 30, no. 4:669-84. [Je.] '41. Growth of a group mind in Britain. Julian S. Huxley.

THE EIGHT POINT PROGRAM

BOOKS AND PAMPHLETS

Commission To Study the Organization of Peace. Atlantic charter; eight-point declaration of President Roosevelt and Prime Minister Churchill, August 14, 1941; [and parallel passages from the Preliminary Report of the Commission To Study the Organization of Peace]. 8p. The Commission. 8 W. 40th St. N.Y. D. '41.

*Commission To Study the Organization of Peace. Comment on the eight-point declaration of President Roosevelt and Prime Minister Churchill, August 14, 1941; with study questions and suggested references. 20p. The Commission. 8 W. 40th St. N.Y. D. '41.

Davis, Forrest. Atlantic system; the story of Anglo-American control of the seas. 363p. Reynal & Hitchcock. N.Y. '41.

Dulles, John Foster. Long range peace objectives; including an analysis of the Roosevelt-Churchill eight point declaration. 29p. Commission To Study the Bases of a Just and Durable Peace. 297 4th Av. N.Y. '41.

*Pickard, Bertram. Analysis of the Atlantic charter. 10p. mim. (Bulletin no. 9) Commission To Study the Organization of Peace. 8 W. 40th St. N.Y. S.-N. '41.

Scherman, Harry. Last best hope of earth. 43p. Random House. N.Y. '41.

Waton, Harry. Historic significance of the Roosevelt-Churchill conference. 9p. mim. Committee for the Preservation of the Jews. 381 Van Siclen Av. Brooklyn, N.Y. S. 19, '41.

Welles, Sumner. Post-war commercial policy; address before the National Foreign Trade Convention, October 7, 1941. 10p. (Dept. of State pub. 1660, Commercial Policy ser. 71) Supt. of Docs. Wash. D.C. '41. (F)

PERIODICALS

Amerasia. 5:425-32. D. '41. Goal beyond victory; lessons of Versailles for the future Pacific settlement. Benjamin H. Kizer.

Atlantic Monthly. 168:567-74. N. '41. Last best hope of earth. Harry Scherman.

*Barron's. 21:3. O. 13, '41. Atlantic charter; some consequences if its aims are adopted. James Truslow Adams.

Canadian Forum. 21:164. S. '41. 8 points leading where? (A)

Central European Observer. 18:273-4. O. 3, '41. Europe to be. H. Wickham Steed.

China Weekly Review. 97:355-6. Ag. 23, '41. Eight points; with text of Roosevelt-Churchill declaration.

China Weekly Review. 97:370. Ag. 23, '41. World-wide reactions to the joint declaration of President Roosevelt and Mr. Churchill.

Christian Century. 58:1046-7. Ag. 27, '41. Eight points.

Christian Century. 58:1102-4. S. 10, '41. Christians and an armed world order. (A)

Christian Century. 58:1276-7. O. 15, '41. Missionaries on the eight points. (F)

Conscience (India). 3:337-8. S. 18, '41. Eight-point plan and Hitler's new order.

Contemporary Review. 161:1-8. Ja. '42. Thoughts on the Atlantic charter. Viscount Samuel. (F)

Co-operative Review (England). 15:331-2. N. '41. Co-operation and the Atlantic charter. J. J. Worley. (A)

Current History. n.s. 1:113-26. O. '41. Roosevelt and Churchill confer; with texts of Roosevelt and Churchill statements. Denna Frank Fleming.

Economist (London). 141:219-20. Ag. 23, '41. War and peace; meeting between Mr. Churchill and President Roosevelt.

Editorial Research Reports. p. 283-302. O. 30, '41. Enforcement of world peace. Buel W. Patch.

Fortune. 25:42-3+. Ja. '42. Peace without platitudes. John Foster Dulles.

Great Britain and the East. 57:115. Ag. 21, '41. Atlantic accord.

Great Britain and the East. 57:143. Ag. 28, '41. Future of export trade; the democracies' eight-point declaration. J. Maurice.

Great Britain and the East. 57:227, 231. O. 9, '41. Indian nonsense; Punjab Premier and Churchill's statement on the Atlantic charter.

*International Conciliation. 372:595-6. S. '41. Joint declaration of peace aims. Franklin D. Roosevelt and Winston Churchill.
  Same. Catholic World. 154:106-7. O. '41; Current History. n.s. 1:121. O. '41; Fortune. 25:43. Ja. '42; Newsweek. 18:13. Ag. 25, '41; United States News. 11:9. Ag. 22, '41. *Same abridged.* School Life. 27:1. O. '41.

Nation. 153:152-3. Ag. 23, '41. Prelude to action; major assumptions for America that underlie the eight points. Freda Kirchwey. (F)

Nation. 153:296-7. O. 4, '41. New charter and allied morale. (F)

Nation. 153:533-5. N. 29, '41. Raw materials hoax. Gabriel Javsicas.

National Review. 117:259-62. S. '41. Mr. Churchill's trip.

National Review. 117:448-56. O. '41. American news. Denys Smith.

Nature. 148:203-5. Ag. 23, '41. World magna charta.

Nature. 148:323-5. S. 20, '41. Colonial development.

New Statesman and Nation. 22:175-6. Ag. 23, '41. Atlantic conference.

New Statesman and Nation. 22:231. S. 6, '41. Eight points. Civis Mundi.

New York Times. p. 3E. Ag. 17, '41. Dramatic talks at sea spike a Hitler peace. Turner Catledge.

New York Times. p. 14. S. 10, '41. Excerpts from speech in House of Commons, September 9, 1941. Winston Churchill.

Newsweek. 18:38. Ag. 25, '41. Economic implications of the eight points. Ralph Robey. (F)

Nineteenth Century. 130:141-9. S. '41. Situation. F. A. Voigt. (A)

Political Quarterly. 12:367-79. O. '41. How to make the peace. Leonard Woolf.

Queen's Quarterly. 48, no. 3:295-9. [Ag.] '41. Atlantic conference; humanitarian document; will the British and American peoples live up to it? B. K. Sandwell.

Saturday Evening Post. 214:26. S. 27, '41. Declaration of the Atlantic.

Scholastic. 39:6, 9-10. S. 15, '41. Two men on a boat; Churchill and Roosevelt issue eight points for future peace.

Scholastic. 39:11-12. S. 29, '41. Freedom of the seas 1941 model.

Spectator (London). 167:171-2. Ag. 22, '41. Atlantic harvest.
    Discussion. Spectator. 167:205, 237. Ag. 29, S. 5, '41.

Spectator (London). 167:230-1. S. 5, '41. Fourteen and eight. Wilson Harris.

Spectator (London). 167:251-2. S. 12, '41. Europe of tomorrow.

Spectator (London). 167:298. S. 26, '41. Allies and the charter.

Time. 38:23. Ag. 25, '41. Points on the points.

Time. 38:43-4. O. 13, '41. Peace without platitudes; comments of Commission To Study the Bases of a Just and Durable Peace.

Time. 38:14. D. 1, '41. Beyond the horizon.

United States News. 11:7-9. Ag. 22, '41. Roosevelt-Churchill: inside story of meeting.

United States News. 11:18-19. Ag. 22, '41. Eight points. David Lawrence. (F)

Vital Speeches of the Day. 7:674+. S. 1, '41. Somewhere in the Atlantic; radio address, August 24, 1941. Winston Churchill.
Same. International Conciliation. 373:660-7. O. '41; Same. New York Times. p. 4. Ag. 25, '41; Excerpts. Time. 38:11, 21. S. 1, '41; Current History. n.s. 1:123-6. O. '41.

Vital Speeches of the Day. 7:678-9. S. 1, '41. No peace with Hitler; eight common principles for a better world. Franklin D. Roosevelt.
Same. Current History. n.s. 1:121-3. O. '41.

Vital Speeches of the Day. 7:679-80. S. 1, '41. Examination of the eight points; we must not commit ourselves to war. Henry Noble MacCracken.

World Affairs Interpreter. 12:243-6. O. '41. [Eight point program compared with Wilson's fourteen points]. J. Eugene Harley.

*World Affairs Interpreter. 12:367-81. Ja. '42. Atlantic charter. Vlastimil Kybal. (F)

INTERNATIONAL FEDERATION

Books and Pamphlets

Adow, Benjamin. World's international, a vision of the future. 8p. Pamphlet Distributing Co. 313 W. 35th St. N.Y. '41.

American Society of International Law. Proceedings. 1941:100-6, 120-42. International constitutional law; is there an unwritten constitution of the society of nations? with discussion. Amos J. Peaslee.

American Society of International Law. Proceedings. 1941:106-42. International organization; an examination of projected world order plans in comparison with conditions in 1919; with discussion. Egon Ranshofen-Wertheimer.

Armstrong, George Gilbert. Why another world war? how we missed collective security. 224p. George Allen & Unwin. Lond. '41.

Barnes, Harry Elmer and Nash, Vernon. Should the democracies unite in a federal world government? 11p. mim. (Empire State Town Meeting Bulletin. no. 65) Union College Campus. Schenectady, N.Y. F. 9, '41.

Clark, Grenville. Memorandum with regard to a new effort to organize peace and containing a proposal for a federation of free peoples in the form of a draft (with explanatory notes) of a constitution for the proposed federation. 38p. The Author. 31 Nassau St. N.Y. Ja. '40. (F)

Commission To Study the Organization of Peace. Which way to lasting peace? 88p. The Commission. 8 W. 40th St. N.Y. '40.

Coudenhove-Kalergi, R. N. Future of Europe and America. 14p. mim. Institute of Public Affairs. Univ. of Virginia. Charlottesville. Jl. 4, '41. (F)

Dillaway, Newton. For democracy and federation; a reply to Anne Morrow Lindbergh. Newton Dellaway Books, Pub. Reading, Mass. '41. (F)

Federal Union, Inc. Democracy's answer to Hitler; program presented at the United States of the World dinner Jan. 22, 1941, under the auspices of Federal Union, Inc. 42p. The Union. 10 E. 40th St. N.Y. '41. (F)

Federal Union, Inc. What is federal union? 8p. The Union. 10 E. 40th St. N.Y. n.d.

Haile, Pennington. After the war, plans and problems; a summary of views on international organization, Western Hemisphere organization, economic and social reconstruction, and religious and ethical approach. 30p. Carnegie Endowment for International Peace. 405 W. 117th St. N.Y. My. '41.

Heymann, Hans. Plan for permanent peace. 315p. Harper & Bros. N.Y. '41.

Institute of World Affairs. Proceedings. 18:259-65. '40. United States as a guide to world government. Kenneth C. Cole.

Johnsen, Julia E. comp. International federation of democracies (proposed). 263p. (Reference Shelf. Vol. 14, no. 8) H. W. Wilson Co. N.Y. Ap. '41.

Lambert, R. S. Federal union, panacea or delusion? p. 3-12. (Food for Thought no. 11) Canadian Assn. for Adult Education. 198 College St. Toronto. Ja. '41.

League of Nations Association. Educational Committee. Essential facts underlying world organization. 47p. The Association. 8 W. 40th St. N.Y. '40.

Merriam, Charles E. On the agenda of democracy. 135p. Harvard Univ. Press. Cambridge, Mass. '41.

Niemeyer, Gerhart. Organization or orientation. *In* his Law without force. p. 379-402. Princeton Univ. Press. Princeton, N.J. '41.

Purdom, C. B. New order. 286p. J. M. Dent & Sons. Lond. '41.

Ralston, Jackson H. Quest for international order. 205p. John Byrne & Co. Wash. D.C. '41.

Robinson, Howard. Toward international organization. 13p. mim. Publicity Bureau. Oberlin College. Oberlin, O. O. 9, '41.

Scandrett, Richard B. Jr. Divided they fall; a plea for unity. 76p. Harper & Bros. N.Y. '41.

Warburg, James P. Isolationist illusion and world peace. 32p. (America in a World at War no. 11) Farrar & Rinehart. N.Y. '41.

Wilson, Duncan and Wilson, Elizabeth. Federation and world order. 184p. Thomas Nelson & Sons. N.Y. '40.

Wootton, Barbara and Hardy, E. Should socialists support federal union? report of a debate. 46p. (S.P.G.B. Library no. 14) Socialist Party of Great Britain. 42 Great Dover St. Lond. S.E. 1. My. 6, '40.

World Citizens Association. World's destiny and the United States; a conference of experts in international relations. 309p. The Association. 84-86 E. Randolph St. Chic. '41.

PERIODICALS

American Mercury. 53:546-51. N. '41. Union now with Germany; immediate formation of free German state as weapon against Nazi rule. Hubertus Loewenstein.

*American Political Science Review. 35:1120-7. D. '41. Political basis of federation. William P. Maddox.

American Scholar. 10, no. 4:402-9. [O.] '41. World government today and tomorrow. Amos J. Peaslee.

Annals of the American Academy. 216:125-34. Jl. '41. Economic union and enduring peace. Otto Tod Mallery.

Annals of the American Academy. 216:140-9. Jl. '41. America seen from abroad. Arthur Sweetser.

Annals of the American Academy. 218:132-40. N. '41. Prospect for a union of democracies. W. Menzies Whitelaw.

Annals of the American Academy. 218:153-61. N. '41. Future of nationalism and the nation-state. Percy E. Corbett.

Antioch Review. 1:21-34. Mr. '41. War aims. Henry G. Alsberg.

Asia. 41:403. Ag. '41. Union now, with Asia. Walter Brooks Foley. (F)

Asia. 41:524. S. '41. No union without China! Pearl S. Buck.
Discussion. Asia. 41:597. N. '41.

Atlantic Monthly. 168:584-7. N. '41. Beware the aftermath. A. Lawrence Lowell.

China Weekly Review. 97:109-10. Je. 28, '41. Sassoon, Hore-Belisha revive the idea of a federal union.

Christian Century. 58:974-6. Ag. 6, '41. Thinking of peace; discussion of Sumner Welles' address at the dedication of a new wing of the Norwegian legation.

Christian Century. 58:1139-41. S. 17, '41. America united, on what level? E. Stanley Jones.

Christian Century. 59:139-41. F. 4, '42. What kind of peace? Walter W. Van Kirk.

Christian Science Monitor Weekly Magazine Section. p. 7+. S. 27, '41. Case for world union. Ralph G. Lindstrom. (F)

Common Sense. 10:182-3+. Je. '41. Federalism vs. totalitarianism. Denis de Rougemont.

Commonweal. 34:510-12. S. 19, '41. What Switzerland teaches: federalism and regionalism for man's freedom; excerpt from The Heart of Europe. Denis de Rougemont and Charlotte Muret.

Congressional Record. 88:A488-9. F. 9, '42. Editor's notebook. John S. Knight.

Events. 9:241-8, 321-30, 435-43. Ap.-Je. '41. Problems of peace settlement. Sidney B. Fay.

Federal Union World. Formerly Union Now Bulletin. Emery W. Balduf, ed. Federal Union, Inc. 10 E. 40th St. N.Y.

Federal Union World. 3:1-2+, 3-5. S.-N '41. World government ahead? which kind? Irving Fisher.

Free Europe (London). 4:186. S. 19, '41. Political example of the British commonwealth. Donald Cowie.

Harvard Guardian. 6:16-19. O. '41. In pursuit of a sound peace. Stanwood Kenyon.

Independent Woman. 20:323+. N. '41. After the war, what? Lewis L. Lorwin.

Institute of International Education News Bulletin. 17:3-5. N. '41. Sovereignty. Stephen P. Duggan.

Modern Industry. 2:52-5+. N. '41. Would a federal union of democracies benefit free enterprise? a debate. Patrick Welch; J. D. Holtzermann.

Nation. 153:473-4. N. 15, '41. Federation is not enough. Norman Angell.

New Europe. 1:263-5. S. '41. Some trends in European federalism. Felix Gross.

New Republic. 105:253-4. Ag. 25, '41. Union of the democracies. Borden Helmer.

New Republic. 105:460-2. O. 13, '41. U powers; United Kingdom, United States and USSR. Julian Huxley.

New York Times Magazine. p. 3+. Jl. 13, '41. If we had joined the League there might not have been a Hitler. Edwin L. James.

New York Times. p. 16. O. 11, '41. Union for peace urged now. W. N. Findley. (F)

New York Times. p. 1, 4. Ja. 3, '42. 26 nations join in anti-Axis pact.

Political Quarterly. 12:121-33. Ap. '41. Resurrection of the League; review of A Great Experiment, the autobiography of Viscount Cecil. H. Lauterpacht.

Quarterly Journal of Economics. 56:49-92. N. '41. Tariff aspects of a federal union. John S. De Beers.

Quarterly Review. 277:27-43. Jl. '41. Problems of federalism. J. A. R. Marriott.

Spectator (London). 166:419-20. Ap. 18, '41. Indian tangle and world federation; review of Unity of India, by J. Nehru. Arthur Moore.

Twice a Year. no. 7:185-238. Fall '41. Federalism: patterns of unification in Europe. Hans Fried.

Virginia Quarterly Review. 17, no. 4:491-501. [O.] '41. Idea of a federation. Denis de Rougemont.

World Affairs. 104:231-4. D. '41. World organization and the American continent. Ricardo J. Alfaro. (F)

World Federation—Now; official organ of the Campaign for World Government. William B. Lloyd, Jr., ed. 166 W. Jackson Blvd. Chic.

ANGLO-AMERICAN UNION

BOOKS AND PAMPHLETS

Boyd, Julian P. Anglo-American union; Joseph Galloway's plans to preserve the British Empire, 1774-1788. 185p. Univ. of Pennsylvania Press. Phila. '41.

Catlin, George E. G. One Anglo-American nation; the foundations of Anglo-Saxony as basis of world federation; a British response to Streit. 155p. Macmillan Co. Toronto. '41.

Day, Stephen A. We must save the republic. 128p. Shaw Pub. Co. Wash. D.C. '41. (A)

Day, Stephen A.; Mundt, Karl E.; Streit, Clarence K.; and Kingdon, Frank. Shall the United States form now a federal union with the British Commonwealth? 15p. (American Forum of the Air. Vol. 3, no. 31) Ransdell, Inc. Wash. D.C. Ag. 3, '41.

Hall, H. Duncan. Anglo-American nucleus of world order. 8p. mim. Institute of Public Affairs. Univ. of Virginia. Charlottesville. Jl. 4, '41. (F)

MacCormac, John. Pax Britamericana—or none. 10p. mim. American Institute of Public Affairs. Univ. of Virginia. Charlottesville. Je. 24, '41. (F)

Mowrer, Edgar Ansel. World or the Western Hemisphere. 12p. mim. Institute of Public Affairs. Univ. of Virginia. Charlottesville. Je. 24, '41. (F)

National Planning Association. United States' cooperation with the British nations; a survey of present relations and their post-war implications. 51p. (Planning Pamphlets no. 6) The Association. 1721 Eye St. N.W. Wash. D.C. Ag. '41.

Nichols, Egbert Ray, ed. Union for defense of the Western hemisphere. *In* his Intercollegiate debates. Vol. 22. p. 155-98. Noble & Noble. N.Y. '41.
Bibliography. p. 191-8.

Phelps, Edith M. ed. Union of the United States and the British Commonwealth of Nations. *In* her University debaters' annual, 1940-1941. p. 243-80. H. W. Wilson Co. N.Y. '41.

PERIODICALS

American Mercury. 52:666-76. Je. '41. Blueprint for an enduring peace. Bertrand Russell. (F)
Discussion. American Mercury. 53:251-2. Ag. '41.

American Scholar. 11, no. 1:45-58. [Ja.] '42. England and the English-speaking people. John Erskine.

Annals of the American Academy. 216:150-5. Jl. '41. American relations with Britain. William Hard.

Christian Science Monitor Weekly Magazine Section. p. 6+. Ag. 23, '41. Toward an Anglo-American new order. Tracy Hollingsworth Lay. (F)

Christian Science Monitor Weekly Magazine Section. p. 1-2. S. 6, '41. Superstate; one dominant force must emerge from this conflict. Tracy Hollingsworth Lay. (F)

Collier's. 108:62. Jl. 19, '41. Team up with Britain now? latest union now proposal.

Congressional Digest. 20:163-92. Je. '41. Proposed union of the world's democracies; fact material and pro and con discussion.

Congressional Record. 87:A2531-4. My. 20, '41. Union now—the latest subversive activity in America. Paul W. Shafer. (A)

Congressional Record. 88:A361-2. F. 2, '42. Union now—reasons are given why plan would be impractical. Archibald E. Stevenson. (A)

Decision. 1:17-25. Mr. '41. Federal union; a debate on the Streit plan. Alfred M. Bingham; Clarence K. Streit and Patrick Welch.

Economist (London). 140:649-51. My. 17, '41. Union now with America?
Same slightly condensed. New Republic. 104:880-2. Je. 30, '41. British view of union now.

Federal Union World. 3:1+. Je. '41. Is union with Britain constitutional? Paul G. Steinbicker.

Foreign Affairs. 19:727-8. Jl. '41. Atlantic area. Francis Pickens Miller.

THE "EIGHT POINTS" 123

Foreign Affairs. 20:1-17. O. '41. Anglo-American pitfalls. Geoffrey Crowther.

International Conciliation. 375:715-20. D. '41. Next armistice, and after. Douglas Johnson.

Living Age. 360:310-20. Je. '41. Short cut to union now; pro and con. Rubin Gotesky; Sidney Hertzberg.

Living Age. 360:402-3. Jl. '41. Movement for some form of Anglo-American union has progressed far beyond the shores of the United States.

Nation. 153:70-2. Jl. 26, '41. Federal union in Britain. Barbara Wootton. (F)

Nature. 147:517-19. My. 3, '41. Anglo-American collaboration for democracy.

Nature. 148:61-3. Jl. 19, '41. Anglo-American collaboration.

New Europe. 1:127-9, 148-50. Ap.-My. '41. Problem of the supernational state. Alexander Hertz.

New Republic. 105:297-300. S. 8, '41. Substitute for imperialism.

New Statesman and Nation. 22:119-20. Ag. 2, '41. America leading; review of Union now with Britain, by C. K. Streit. Freda White. *Discussion.* New Statesman and Nation. 22:138, 160. Ag. 9-16. '41.

New York Times. p. 8E. Je. 29, '41. Our union with Britain suggested; Adam Smith's plan of federation viewed as more feasible now than when it was first promulgated in 1776. Oscar Jaszi.

New York Times. p. 22. Ja. 6, '42. Federal union suggested. Lyman Beecher Stowe. (F)

New York Times. p. 22. Ja. 6, '42. Union principle opposed. Merwin K. Hart. (A)

New York Times. p. 6E. Ja. 25, '42. United nations council. Clarence K. Streit. (F)

Political Quarterly. 12:214-22. Ap. '41. Towards a regional empire. Donald Cowie.

Political Quarterly. 12:431-41. O. '41. Anglo-American co-operation. George W. Keeton. (F)

Progressive Education. 18:283-4. O. '41. United democracies. Clarence K. Streit. (F)

Reader's Digest. 39:77-82. Jl. '41. Union of the English-speaking democracies now? pro and con.

Saturday Evening Post. 214:24. O. 25, '41. Whose America?

Saturday Evening Post. 214:26. F. 7, '42. Anglo-American unity.

Scribner's Commentator. 9:19-22. Mr. '41. Union now, for what? Howard M. Yates. (A)

Scribner's Commentator. 9:17-21. My. '41. Union now, by C. K. Streit; review. Albert J. Nock. (A)

Scribner's Commentator. 10:51-3. Jl. '41. Times have changed; George Washington interviews Clarence Streit; one-act play. Eleanor Hart. (A)

Scribner's Commentator. 11:45-9. D. '41. Treason is fashionable. George H. Cless, Jr. (A)

Spectator (London). 166:611. Je. 6, '41. Federal dream; review of Union now with Britain, by C. K. Streit. Allan Nevins.
   Discussion. Spectator. 166:599, 656. Je. 6, 20, '41.

REGIONAL ORGANIZATION AND PROBLEMS

BOOKS AND PAMPHLETS

Felix, Archduke of Austria. Danubian solution. 10p. mim. Institute of Public Affairs. Univ. of Virginia. Charlottesville. Jl. 4, '41.

MacKay, R. W. G. Peace aims and the new order. 306p. Dodd, Mead & Co. N.Y. '41.

Manden, Linden A. Regional international organization. *In* his Foundations of modern world society. p. 798-874. Stanford Univ. Press. Stanford University, Calif. '41.

Nichols, Egbert Ray, ed. Federation of English-speaking nations. *In* his Intercollegiate debates. Vol. 22. p. 49-87. Noble & Noble. N.Y. '41.
   Bibliography. p. 83-7.

Phelps, Edith M. ed. Western hemisphere defense. *In* University debaters' annual, 1940-1941. p. 451-513. H. W. Wilson Co. N.Y. '41.
   Bibliography. p. 500-13.

Rankin, E. R. comp. Hemisphere defense; debate handbook. 112p. (Extension Bulletin. Vol. 21, no. 2) Univ. of North Carolina Press. Chapel Hill. S. '41.

PERIODICALS

Asia. 41:327. Jl. '41. Pan-Pacific union for defense, political stability and trade expansion. Edna Lonigan.

Asia. 41:715-18. D. '41. Can the Arab peoples unite? Albert Viton.

Canadian Forum. 21:199-202. O. '41. Pan America in the world order; federal idea has two possible applications. John P. Humphrey.

Catholic World. 44:37-45. O. '41. Key position of Europe; need of a Danubian federation. Karl Traisner.

Catholic World. 154:300-5. D. '41. Can there be peace in Europe? Maximilian Opolony.

Common Sense. 10:296-300. O. '41. America and Europe. R. N. Coudenhove-Kalergi.

Commonweal. 34:540-2. S. 26, '41. Disunion now; plea for a society based upon small autonomous units. Hans Kohr.

Contemporary Review. 160:233-8. O. '41. Central European federation. Milan Hodza.

Contemporary Review. 160:278-82. N. '41. Liberty or uniformity in Eastern Europe. Stefan Osusky.

Current History. n.s. 1:12-15. S. '41. Germany should not be dismembered. Sidney B. Fay.

Foreign Affairs. 19:778-89. Jl. '41. Canada in the western hemisphere. P. E. Corbett.

Foreign Affairs. 20:18-29. O. '41. War for eastern Europe. Bruce Hopper.

Foreign Affairs. 20:226-42. Ja. '42. Organization of post-war Europe. Edvard Benes.

Foreign Affairs. 20:243-52. Ja. '42. Danubian reconstruction. Otto of Austria.

Foreign Affairs. 20:253-65. Ja. '42. Bringing the Monroe Doctrine up to date. Dexter Perkins.

Fortnightly. 156 (n.s. 150):105-12, 249-56, 356-63, 414-21, 538-47. Ag.-D. '41. Planning post-war Europe. J. Emlyn Williams, ed.

Fortnightly. 156 (n.s. 150):257-9. S. '41. Dangerous theory. Z. Grabowski.

Fortune. 24:94-7. D. '41. Europe: we missed the point; for twenty years we have misread European history.

Harvard Law Review. 55:561-94. F. '42. European federation—the democratic alternative. Arnold Brecht.

Hibbert Journal. 40:1-14. O. '41. End of the balance of power, what is to succeed? F. H. Heinemann.

Inter-American Quarterly. 3:5-13. O. '41. Twenty-second chair: is it for Canada? John P. Humphrey.

Menorah Journal. 29:241-8. O. '41. Design for peace. Zakkaius.

Menorah Journal. 29:249-65. O. '41. Unity of Europe. Albert Guerard.

New Europe. 1:117-21. Ap. '41. Federation for Eastern Europe. By a Group of U.S. Military Experts.

New Europe. 2:47-50. Ja. '42. Regionalism versus universalism. Felix Gross.

New York Times. p. 7E. N. 23, '41. Looking forward; three courses seen for us in move for peace. R. N. Coudenhove-Kalergi.

Queen's Quarterly. 48, no. 4:329-41. [N.] '41. Europe wants a strong Britain. H. Noel Fieldhouse.

Rotarian. 60:8-11. Ja. '42. Americas show the way. Walter B. Pitkin.

UNIVERSITY DEBATERS' ANNUALS

E. M. PHELPS, Ed. *Cloth. Price* $2.25

Series of year books, each a collection of representative intercollegiate debates on important questions of the day. Constructive and rebuttal speeches for both sides. Each debate is accompanied by selected bibliography and briefs.